The Iron Saint

© 2022 Simon Webb

The right of Simon Webb to be identified as the Author of the Work has been asserted by him in accordance with the Copyright, Designs and Patents Act 1988. All rights reserved.

Published by The Langley Press, 2022

The picture on page six is a detail of Albrecht Dürer's woodcut of a rhinoceros.

This book is dedicated to the memory of my friend, Joan Cuthbertson

The Iron Saint

The Life and Times of Godric of Finchale

Simon Webb

Also from the Langley Press

The Legend of Saint Cuthbert
In Search of the Northern Saints
In Search of the Celtic Saints
In Search of Bede
Bede's Life of Cuthbert
The Legend of Saint Edmund
The Voyage of Saint Brendan
The Legend of Saint Edmund
In Search of Saint Alban
A Little Book of English Saints
The Life and Times of Paul Cuffe
The Life and Times of Jeremiah Dixon
John Lilburne: Gentleman, Leveller, Quaker

For more books from the Langley Press, please visit our website at:

www.langleypress.co.uk

Contents

Visitors	7
Norfolk and Everywhere Else	20
The King of Jerusalem	28
The Road to Finchale	47
St Giles and St Mary	55
The Hermit's Life	62
Finchale at Last	73
War and Miracles	85
Monks, Music and More Miracles	95
Buechner's Book	106
What Godric Was	116
Appendix: Godric's Songs	123
Bibliography	125

Like the wild deer that feeds wherever it likes,
The wise man loves freedom, and wanders alone,
A rhino in the forest.

from The Rhinoceros Sutra

Visitors

It was probably some time in 1138 that a band of marauding Scots came across a strange, handmade-looking group of buildings by the River Wear at Finchale near Durham. The Scots, who were certainly armed and may have worn kilts, probably expected the isolated dwelling between the river and the forest to be deserted. Since their king, David I of Scotland, had invaded that summer, many of the English had fled their homes with as many of their valuables as they could carry. But at some point in their visit, the Caledonian visitors encountered the occupant of the riverside retreat, who probably looked as strange to them as his home did.

Perhaps Godric came upon them when they were searching his buildings for any valuables. Or maybe they had pulled up some of the food he was growing, or found food he had stored, and were enjoying an impromptu meal at their host's expense. In any case the men from north of the border saw a short, barefoot, stocky man in his early seventies, who by this time may have been wearing a paradoxical get-up: an iron tunic over a black monk's habit. By twelfth-century standards, Godric was by this time a very old man, yet he was permanently camped out by a river in the north of England, with few if any creature comforts. Had his visitors ever seen such a robust old fellow?

Did they think Godric was some elderly soldier, who had deserted the main body of the English army and was now hiding away like an outlaw in this wild, wooded place? Did they think that the old man thought he could drive them away, with his armour and his staff? They decided to subject the sturdy old man to a prolonged beating, and set about desecrating his DIY chapel, pouring out the communion wine and trampling the bread underfoot.

Godric must have had long hair, and perhaps a long beard, because, according to his friend and biographer Reginald of Durham, his impolite visitors twisted a stout stick into his grey locks, to act as a handle while they prepared to cut off his head. Where was his treasure? they demanded. Whatever language they used, it is likely that the hermit's definition of the word 'treasure' was different to theirs.

At this stage in the proceedings, most victims of this kind of treatment would be soiling themselves, screaming, sobbing, or all of the above. The Scots were amazed to see that their elderly host remained calm, even serene, meekly stretching out his neck to meet their blade, and martyrdom. Sensing that their intended victim might be something more than just another poor old man, the largest and strongest of the Scots saved Godric's life by driving out his murderous companions.

They left their victim battered, and traumatised by the desecration of his sacred space, but still alive. The story goes that none of the men who attacked Godric that day lived long enough to get home. One went mad, bit out his own tongue and as a result probably bled to death. Another committed suicide by throwing himself into the River Wear. Those medieval chroniclers seemed to enjoy relating the wretched lives and gruesome deaths of the enemies of the saints: William de Tracey, one of the murderers of Thomas Becket, was said to have contracted leprosy. Unlike his doomed tormentors, Saint Godric of Finchale lived to a very great age.

Most of the older sources for Godric and his period in England are Latin chronicles written by monks, or others in holy orders. Because surnames had not been established at the time, many of these authors are identified by their first names, followed by the name of a place with which they are associated. Their number includes Geoffrey of Monmouth, William of Malmesbury, Henry of Huntingdon, Roger of Hoveden, John of Worcester; and Simeon and Reginald, both of Durham. When death or some other reason forced these chroniclers to break off their histories, they were often continued by other authors, some of whom were anonymous.

Although their works supply invaluable insights into European history, monkish chroniclers like Reginald were not historians in the modern sense, and they often betrayed their religious background by promoting a very Christian perspective. For modern tastes, they can attach too much importance to religious events such as the election of a new bishop or the death of a pope, and they sometimes attribute the success or failure of, say, a king, to factors such as the piety of the monarch, and not his wealth, military prowess or general good sense.

Because their chronicles are in a sense Christian propaganda, the monkish chroniclers can sometimes embroider or exaggerate events, especially visions and miracles, in an attempt to renew their readers' dedication to the faith. They are certainly not even-handed about other faiths, or alternative versions of Christianity. Bede's obsession with the correct calculation of Easter almost spoils parts of his *Ecclesiastical History* for some modern readers. He sometimes seems to reject the whole inspiring edifice of Celtic Christianity, in favour of the Latin variety that then dominated much of western Europe, simply because the Catholics calculated the date of Easter using a method of which he approved. For Bede, the celebration of Easter on the 'wrong' day was a theological scandal.

In Durham itself, Simeon, Reginald and other chroniclers must sometimes have felt overshadowed by the reputation of Bede, the eighth-century scholar-saint whose body lay, and still lies, in the city's cathedral. The medieval chronicler *par excellence*, Bede wrote his celebrated *Ecclesiastical History*, as well as a *Life* of Saint Cuthbert (who also sleeps in Durham Cathedral) and various other works, not only of history, but also of theology, biblical exegesis and science.

In 1845 Durham's venerable Surtees Society published an edition of Reginald's *Life* of Godric in the original Latin. In his preface the prolific editor, author and translator Joseph Stevenson explored the various sources for the saint's life, of which he asserted that Reginald's final text was the most important. From the existence of two manuscripts comprising shorter versions of Godric's story, Stevenson arrived at the idea that the text he printed was a copy of a final, long version by Reginald, which was preceded by less extensive accounts by the same author.

The shorter versions are still extant in the British Library's collection. The third, longer version, which Stevenson used, is at Oxford. Stevenson also mentioned a biography of Godric by Germanus, who was prior of Durham during part of Godric's life, and was apparently very intimate with the saint. Unfortunately, only fragments of this biography exist, as excerpts copied into another book by a monk called Geoffrey of Durham. If we count the three versions of Godric's life that Stevenson attributed to Reginald, then it appears that Durham alone produced no less than five biographies of the hermit of Finchale, that we know of.

In those days, the authors of these works would not have been criticised for depending on previous accounts, or revisiting hoary old material. The *literati* of the Middle Ages thought little of originality, and preferred their authors to rely on earlier authorities.

The Oxford manuscript of Reginald's fullest version that Stevenson used was, he believed, copied out in an 'elegant hand' on vellum by one Swalwell, a monk of Durham who died shortly before the Dissolution of the Monasteries by King Henry VIII; a grim process which began in 1536. The fact that a sixteenth-century scribe (or his master) should have considered such a project worthwhile perhaps attests to the value still placed on Godric's memory at Durham over three hundred years after the hermit's death. That Reginald himself may have written three distinct versions of his own narrative suggests either that he thought the task was worth re-visiting, or that someone else was spurring him on to expand his account, or both.

Reginald's text has all the flaws of the monkish chroniclers of the period, together with some very turgid Latin and an annoying neglect of the important business of telling the reader exactly when certain events happened. Sometimes it is necessary to try to date events by details in the story: there is none of Bede's insistence, seen repeatedly in his *Ecclesiastical History*, on telling us at least the precise year when he believed something occurred. When dealing with the attempts of the Romans to invade Britain, Bede sometimes even tells us how many years before or after the birth of Jesus an event happened, and also the number of years after the foundation of Rome. Later in his narrative, he sometimes gives us BC and AD, as well as the regnal year of a specific king, pope or bishop; i.e. how many years into their reign something took place.

The proliferation of early accounts of Godric may have happened because his memory was respected, and the authors and their masters remembered the saint fondly. They may also have been motivated by a desire to publicise the life of a local holy man – something that might reflect well on Durham, and the monks of Durham who had supported the old man, particularly in his later years. The tomb or grave of a saint conferred prestige on any place in Christendom, and would attract pilgrims, the tourists of the day, who could be a handy source of income for the local church.

Godric died in May 1170: in December of the same year, Thomas Becket was murdered inside Canterbury Cathedral. The ever-popular Saint Cuthbert, buried at Durham, now had some serious competition. Were Durham's attempts to popularise Godric intended in part as a way to divert attention from Canterbury?

The rivalry between Durham and Canterbury comes to the fore in parts of Reginald's narrative. Where he gives details of healing miracles that happened at Finchale after Godric's death, the author sometimes includes episodes where the people needing to be healed are seen to waste their time by visiting Canterbury first. Sometimes they are reprimanded by their friends, or even the spirit of Thomas Becket himself, who upbraids them for wasting their time making a pilgrimage to Canterbury, when Godric's home was so well-known for miraculous cures. Sometimes it is implied that people seeking cures should certainly visit Godric's tomb at Finchale if they live in any part of the north of Great Britain, rather that schlepping all the way down to Kent. Reginald also gives accounts of sick people who were partly cured by visits to other shrines, but were finally and completely healed by Godric's posthumous influence.

Reginald tries to have his cake and eat it too by attempting to link Godric and Becket, and thus cash in on Becket's saintly prestige, while casting shade on Becket's cult in other parts of his narrative. Unfortunately, Reginald's attempts to connect the two saints come over as rather threadbare and unconvincing. They never actually met, but Godric's monkish biographer insists that they communicated with each other via messengers. Reginald also claims that, thanks to his gifts for prophecy and for seeing events at a distance, the hermit of Finchale was able to follow Becket's dramatic, international career without straying from his riverside retreat.

English saints were promoted by the national church out of a kind of pious patriotism, and the hope that miracles and saintliness really could remain features of life many centuries after Jesus preached in Jerusalem, and many thousands of miles from the Holy Land. The fact that several accounts of Godric's life were written before the invention of printing and the introduction of cheap paper is particularly significant, given that the hand-written books of the period were very expensive to produce. The five hundred and sixteen vellum (or parchment) pages of the Lindisfarne Gospels required the skins of around one hundred and fifty calves. Those celebrated Latin Gospels, annotated in the Anglo-Saxon language, were already over three hundred years old by the time Godric was born.

The version of Reginald's *Life* of Godric that Stevenson used is Bodleian Manuscript Laud Misc. 413. This had been owned by two seventeenth-century prebendaries of Durham Cathedral, the second of whom, Augustine Lindsell, gave it to William Laud, who was then Archbishop of Canterbury. The book containing Reginald's *Godric* was among over twelve hundred manuscripts donated by Laud to Oxford's Bodleian Library between 1635 and 1641.

Reginald claimed that he had been asked to write a life of Godric by Aelred (or Ailred) of Rievaulx. Books written at the bidding of a specific person are a long tradition in the Christian Church. Saint Luke, or whoever wrote Luke's Gospel and the New Testament Book of Acts, implies at the beginning of each of these books that they were written at the behest of a mysterious character called Theophilus. Likewise, Aelred himself wrote his *Life* of Saint Ninian at the bidding of, perhaps, a bishop of Galloway in south-west Scotland.

References to patrons or others who had insisted they write a specific work were a way for medieval writers to assert their humility. In the preface to his *Life* of Edward the Confessor, written at the behest of Laurence, abbot of Westminster, Aelred describes himself as useless and foolish. He fears that his feeble writing style will obscure rather than illuminate the life of the saint-king, a subject that Cicero himself would find daunting. Aelred is therefore puzzled by Laurence's request, but proceeds out of faith and love.

In most cases, works were 'commissioned' by people higher up in the pious pecking-order than the author. The lofty position of the 'commissioner' could confer extra kudos on the resulting work. Aelred's *Mirror of Charity*, a guide for novice monks, was commissioned by Bernard of Clairvaux, the celebrated champion of the Cistercian way, and Aelred himself became known as the 'Bernard of the north'.

A letter from Bernard to Aelred has survived, in which the former uses every argument he can think of to overcome the latter's reluctance to write what became his *Mirror of Charity*. Bernard praises Aelred's humility, but urges him not to forget the virtue of obedience. He reminds him of one of the advantages of writing something suggested by someone else: if the resulting text is terrible, some of the blame might be shared by the author's patron.

It is unlikely that a Durham monk like Reginald, however great his independent spirit and literary pretensions, would have refused a request to write a book from a man like Aelred. Although as abbot of Rievaulx, a Cistercian house, he would have had no direct authority over Reginald, a Durham Benedictine, Aelred was an influential man, a friend of kings, princes and bishops, and an important author in his own right. He was born in 1110 at Hexham, roughly thirty-five miles to the north-west of Durham, which means that he may have been in his mid-fifties when he asked Reginald to write his *Life* of Godric.

Aelred had become abbot of the Cistercian monastery at Rievaulx in 1147. Some years before he asked Reginald to tackle the subject of Godric, he had written the aforementioned *Life* of Ninian, the fifth-century 'apostle of the southern Picts'. The abbot also wrote about King Edward the Confessor, King David I of Scotland (who is also regarded as a saint) and the saints of his home town, Hexham. As we shall see, he also wrote on secular subjects, such as the 1138 Scottish invasion of the north of England, and the genealogy of the English kings.

Aelred's international reputation and influence made him the most distinguished visitor to drop in on Godric at Finchale. They enjoyed a long conversation in private, but, sadly, what they said to each other was not recorded.

If Reginald's prior and the then bishop of Durham had supported Aelred's idea, Reginald would have been pretty much obliged to write a *Life* of Godric. It may be that he found the prospect daunting. At that time the best source for Godric was Godric himself, but interviewing him would mean long sessions with the hermit deep in his woodland habitat, which was said to be infested with wolves and snakes. It may be that by this time Reginald had already been visiting, or even living with, the hermit for some time, but in any case his personal, and now literary, involvement with Godric meant that Reginald had to spend a lot of time out of his own natural habitat, the cloisters of Durham priory.

Whatever Reginald's feelings about the project, Godric himself was not keen when the idea of a biography was first put to him. In a shocking outburst, the hermit implied that he was not fit to be the subject of a book. He was fat and coarse, lecherous and dirty. He was no better than a dead flea, a smelly old dog, or a worm. Before he had found religion, he had been a liar, a cheat, a pimp, and a usurer (one who lent money at interest, which was forbidden to Christians). It was several months before Godric calmed down and consented to tell Reginald the story of his life.

There was no full translation into English of Reginald's text until Oxford published Margaret Coombe's version in 2022. It may be that until Coombe, would-be translators have been put off by the monk's difficult Latin. In 1994 Francis Rice, who had been the parish priest of St Godric's Roman Catholic church in Durham for a quarter of a century, published his *Hermit of Finchale*, an account of the saint's life with translations of many extracts from Reginald. Unfortunately this useful book, which runs to over three hundred pages and features illustrations by Mike Attewell, has now become rare.

Readers who manage to get hold of a copy will be forgiven for skipping Rice's last chapter, 'Saint Godric and the Modern World': here the author offers very little useful extra information about Godric, but writes at length about how the modern world is going to hell in a hand-cart. One indicator of this, Rice implies, is the way that gay people are now treated with respect.

Reginald died around 1190: Godric had died twenty years earlier. Since Aelred died in 1167, he cannot have 'commissioned' Reginald to write about Godric after that date, when Godric himself was still alive and had several more years left to live. If we assume that Aelred made his request to Reginald around 1165, then the contemporary bishop of Durham would have been Hugh Pudsey. Hugh, a nephew of the unfortunate King Stephen, was bishop for over forty years, until his death in 1195. He built the exquisite Galilee chapel at the western end of Durham Cathedral, and was a patron of the chronicler Roger of Hoveden. The prior of Durham at the time was Germanus who, as we have seen, also wrote a *Life* of Godric, which now only survives in fragments.

Joseph Stevenson's edition of Reginald's Latin *Life* of Godric has continued to be the ultimate source for accounts of Godric of Finchale right into the twenty-first century. These secondary accounts include an article in the British *Dictionary of National Biography*, entries in collections of hagiographies (or saints' lives) and an entry in Grove, the celebrated reference work on music.

Godric is treated as a rather ridiculous figure by the seventeenth-century author Robert Hegge in his *Legend of St Cuthbert*. According to Hegge, Godric's 'Jerkin was of iron, of which suits of apparel he wore out three in the time of his hermitage, a strange coat, whose stuff had the ironmonger for the draper and a smith for the tailor'.

Hegge also tells us that Godric had a copy of the psalms constantly hanging from his little finger, 'which with use was ever after crooked'. Reginald agrees that the hermit had a crooked finger, but does not suggest that he kept the psalms dangling from it. Hegge's version of Godric enjoys and is not 'affrighted' by the devil, who acts 'Proteus before him', changing into strange shapes that others would find terrifying. The *Legend* also includes a story of a wide-of-the-mark prophesy that originated with Godric. He is supposed to have told Bishop Hugh Pudsey that he (the bishop) would be blind for seven years before his death.

Hugh took this to mean that he would not have to start to repent and reform himself until he went blind, when he would have seven years to live in sackcloth and ashes. As it turned out, Pudsey never went blind, and therefore, some might say, he 'died unprovided for death'. Hegge asserts, however, that the good deeds of the bishop meant that when he died he was 'not in debt for his sins'. The *Legend* has it that these good deeds included building two 'hospitals' (meaning almshouses), the construction of Elvet Bridge over the Wear at Durham, and also putting up the aforementioned Galilee Chapel at Durham Cathedral. This last was started just a few years after the death of Godric in 1170.

It was also Bishop Pudsey (or de Puiset) who founded Finchale Priory near the site of Godric's hermitage. Since the ruins of his foundation have long been a tourist attraction, there have been a succession of slender guide-books that touch on the hermit's life. In a highly eccentric guide published in the 1950s, J.F.J. Smith, who then lived at Finchale Abbey Farm, revealed what he himself had uncovered of the site after a great deal of amateur and perhaps rather haphazard digging, in which he was assisted by volunteers.

Smith seems to have believed that Godric, his story and his riverside home deserved far more attention than they are ever likely to get, even from local Christians. The author dreamed of using Godric as a sort of saintly standard behind which troops of the faithful might rally, before setting off to fight against the evils of communism.

As well as not respecting his neighbour Godric as much as he felt they should, Smith thought that by his time there had already been a long, sad tradition of people misunderstanding details of, for instance, exactly where the saint's hermitage had actually been. Smith attributed the relative failure (what he calls the 'tragedy') of Finchale Priory to the monks' inability to connect their own endeavours to the memory of Godric's life in a meaningful way. A version of Smith's book is still sold at Finchale.

Signs of the 'failure' of the priory that came to occupy the site after Godric's death can be seen in some of the ruins that remain. By the 1360s the number of monks had dwindled to the point where it was decided that the priory church should be reduced in size. This was done by replacing the line of pillars that separated the nave from the side-aisles with walls. This effectively cut off the side-aisles and made the church unusually narrow. Of course the pillars that had originally separated the side-aisles from the nave were not removed: they were merely engulfed by the new walls. The capitals of some of these pillars have been exposed, and they can now be seen re-emerging from the remaining parts of a wall.

The latest Finchale guidebook, by Peter Ryder, was published by English Heritage, which now controls the site, in 2000. Ryder's full-colour pamphlet features a series of artist's impressions by Peter Dunn, showing how the site looked shortly after Godric's death in 1170, then around 1320, and in 1530. By 1530 the days of

Finchale and of all abbeys and priories in England were well and truly numbered. Soon they would be dissolved on the orders of King Henry VIII. Like Finchale, many became picturesque ruins, the 'bare run'd choirs' of Shakespeare's Sonnet 73, where the poet compares them to leafless autumnal trees 'where late the sweet birds sang'.

Norfolk and Everywhere Else

Godric was born at Walpole (then called 'Hanapol') in Norfolk, perhaps around 1065. His parents, Ailward and Ailwen, were poor farmers who brought him up to be a good Christian. The future hermit and saint had a younger sister called Burcwen and a brother called William. The reader will have noticed that though the names Ailward, Ailwen, Godric and Burcwen are seldom to be met with today, there are Williams everywhere in modern English-speaking countries. The parents' (or godparents') choice of name for the second son may reflect the huge change that took place in England shortly after Godric was born. It was of course in 1066 that the Normans, led by the future King William I, successfully conquered England, ending the reign of our country's Anglo-Saxon kings and giving us a new, French-speaking ruling class. It was shortly after the Conquest that English parents turned their backs on Anglo-Saxon names like Ailward and Ailwen, and started to give their babies names like William, based on the French Guillaume.

Abandonment of Anglo-Saxon first names was not the only effect of the Norman Conquest. For the North Country, where Godric would spend most of his long life, the Conquest led to such widespread devastation that some commentators have used the term 'genocide' in this connection.

In his early years as king of England, the Conqueror was faced with rebellions in many parts of his newly-acquired kingdom. Disgruntled Anglo-Saxon nobles formed alliances with, for instance, the kings of Ireland and Denmark; and Sweyn, the Danish king, even joined an uprising in the north of England. The account of William's response to this threat by the chronicler Orderic Vitalis offers a convincing picture of the difficulty of the campaign, at least for the Normans. As we shall see, what roads there were were often in very poor condition, and some routes could only be taken by journeying through thick forests and crossing rivers that had never been bridged. Orderic relates how William had to funnel his army through narrow, wooded gorges and somehow get them across treacherous, undrained marshes.

In this wild landscape it was easy for the rebels to evade William, and he decided to break their spirits but cutting off their food supply. Crops, stores and cattle were callously burned, as were the very tools needed to till the land. As Orderic wrote:

There followed, consequently, so great a scarcity in England in the ensuing years, and severe famine involved the innocent and unarmed population in so much misery, that, in a Christian nation, more than a hundred thousand souls, of both sexes and all ages, perished of want. (trans. Forester, 1853)

Given that the population of England was probably around two million at the time, the famine William had deliberately brought about may have killed a staggering five percent of the Conqueror's new subjects, if Orderic's figure of one hundred thousand dead is to be trusted. The famine may have continued for as long as nine years, and in parts of the north three-quarters of the population either died or became refugees in their own country. This man-made disaster is usually referred to as 'the harrying of the north'.

King William felt the need to harry the north again after Bishop Walcher of Durham, who had been hand-picked by the Conqueror, was murdered by a mob at Gateshead in 1080. According to Simeon of Durham, on this occasion 'nearly the whole land' of Durham was turned 'into a wilderness'. Even innocent locals who had had no part in the events at Gateshead were 'beheaded as criminals, or mutilated by the loss of some of their members'.

Although Godric was born in Norfolk, at some point his family moved to Spalding in Lincolnshire. One day while Godric was wandering alone by the shore, he saw three dolphins stranded on a sand-bank. One of them was dead; the other two were still alive. The youngster claimed the dead one as food, and started to carry it, slung over his shoulder. But the tide was coming in, and Godric was soon up to his neck. He did, not, however, panic, or abandon his dead dolphin. He made the sign of the cross, trusted in God and came safe to shore. His faith saved him, or perhaps his confidence in God prevented him from panicking and flailing about, which might have been particularly dangerous in such circumstances.

The incident recalls a miracle of Cuthbert, the great saint of the North Country. Once when Cuthbert was stranded with some travelling companions on a barren coast in the middle of winter, it began to look as if they might perish from cold and hunger. They could not escape on their ship, because the weather was so atrocious, but Cuthbert prophesied that conditions would soon clear, and told everybody to pray for food. Their prayers were answered when they found some fresh dolphin-meat on the shore, cut up and ready to cook. Cuthbert's dolphin miracle, if such it was, is related in both Bede's biography of the saint, and another, anonymous *Life* of Cuthbert.

Today most people would not dream of eating dolphin, but in medieval times nobody seems to have realised that these intelligent creatures were anything more than just another species of fish.

They could even be eaten on Fridays, when good Christians were supposed to abstain from meat. Apparently dolphin-flesh is very dark and dense, like beef liver, and contains dangerously high levels of mercury.

It seems that Godric was not cut out for the farming life, and when he was barely out of his teens he began to work as a pedlar. We know that he was brave, confident, physically tough, hard-working and good with his hands, and these qualities no doubt helped him to build up the success of his little business, until it became quite a big concern and he was regularly trading with Scotland, Denmark and the Low Countries.

Although, as we know, Godric later accused himself of terrible crimes, his pious upbringing probably meant that even while he had one eye firmly fixed on his burgeoning profits, he always had the other eye anxiously watching the state of his soul. A tender conscience may also have helped him in his work, since his customers, suppliers and any business partners probably felt that here was a merchant that they could trust.

Godric acquired shares in trading vessels, began to skipper ships, and managed to combine business trips with Christian pilgrimages. Reginald tells us that he was an excellent sailor, able to navigate accurately, who could also both read and predict changes in the weather. These abilities may have meant that the ships Godric skippered could sail outside of the normal sailing months, when less bold captains would never dare to set out. It is likely that Godric developed a good sense of the sea's moods because he grew up at Spalding, which was then much nearer the North Sea coast of Lincolnshire. He may have continued to live with his parents at Spalding, at least some of the time: this might, after all, have been a convenient stop during his travels up and down the east coast; and Godric never had a wife to set up an alternative home for him.

In many respects Godric's ascent from farm-boy, to small-time trader, to successful international merchant resembles a similar trajectory followed by the Black American businessman and anti-slavery campaigner Paul Cuffe (1759-1817). Cuffe was also raised near the sea, in his case on the coast of Massachusetts. Like Godric, the American started trading in a small way, then built up his business and acquired useful partners. Cuffe was also physically strong, fearless, enterprising, honest, confident and good with his hands. Like Godric, Paul also skippered some of the ships he owned or part-owned, and proved to be a sound leader and a fine navigator.

True, Cuffe did not give up all his wealth and become a hermit, but he gave time and money to good causes and, unusually for a black man at that time, was accepted as a member of his local Quaker meeting. Like Godric, Cuffe hobnobbed with the great and the good: he may have become the first person of colour to be received as a guest at the White House. Paul was also caught up in larger historical events, becoming an important supporter of a scheme to re-settle American Blacks in Sierra Leone.

At times, Cuffe encountered prejudice, as Godric may have done as an Anglo-Saxon in a country now dominated by the Normans. The Conquest turned people of Godric's ancestry into second-class citizens on their own turf: this is an experience that has been endured by countless indigenous, colonised peoples.

In Britain in the eleventh and twelfth centuries a lot of trade and passenger traffic went around the coast and up and down the navigable rivers, as it would in America in Cuffe's time. In England, this was because the kingdom's roads were so few, and some of them were always in very poor condition. This reliance on water-transport meant that important settlements were often located on the coast, or became river-ports; which made them horribly vulnerable to attack when the Vikings began raiding England late in the eighth century. The Viking raid which is generally accepted as the first ever to affect England also has a link to Saint Cuthbert. This was the horrific 793 C.E. attack on the monastery on the island of Lindisfarne, then the resting-place of Cuthbert's body, which was supposed to have remained miraculously incorrupt for centuries. Repeated raids on such coastal places meant that communities of monks and others withdrew further inland, and Cuthbert's guardians kept the saint's remains at various places including Ripon and Chester-le-Street before they brought them to Durham, where they remain.

Although Godric lived through some violent and tragic times, the threat of Viking raids dwindled significantly around the time that he was born. Shortly before King Harold was felled by a Norman arrow at the Battle of Hastings in October 1066, he had won an important battle against a force of Viking invaders at Stamford Bridge near York. This victory is widely used by historians as the end-point for major Viking incursions into England. It meant that as well as successfully conquering a rich, fertile, well-run country with a temperate climate, King William had also acquired one that had recently been freed from the threat of serious Viking raids, for the first time in nearly three hundred years.

On trading trips up and down the North Sea coast of England and Scotland, Godric got into the habit of visiting sites associated with the seventh-century monk, hermit, bishop and saint, Cuthbert, whom we have already met as the subject of a biography by Bede, and as a saint whose bones once lay in the soil of the island of Lindisfarne. When he visited the islands most closely associated with Cuthbert, Godric would move around on his knees, kiss the ground and prostrate himself.

Although today he is little-known outside of the north-east of England, it is hard to overstate the widespread prestige Cuthbert enjoyed throughout the Middle Ages. Born in Scotland around 634, Cuthbert seems to have come from a noble family: when he turned up at Old Melrose Abbey to offer himself as a novice monk, he arrived on a horse and was carrying a spear – both prestigious possessions.

Cuthbert had turned to the religious life after seeing a vision of the soul of another important local saint, Aidan, rising up to heaven. As a monk, Cuthbert soon became associated with miracles, and was made a prior before he was out of his twenties. He resisted the temptation to stick to his cloister, and was forever out and about among the ordinary people, preaching and performing miracles. He is credited with spectacular cures, and notable victories against the devil.

Driven in part, perhaps, by illness, Cuthbert took up the life of a hermit, eventually on the island of Inner Farne near Lindisfarne, in 676. After eight years as a religious recluse, the saint was persuaded to fill the post of bishop of Lindisfarne. The first bishop of that place had been Aidan, whose soul Cuthbert had seen ascending into heaven in the summer of 651.

Cuthbert served for just under two years as an active, effective and popular bishop, until illness again called him back to his island hermitage. It is likely that Cuthbert's problem was tuberculosis: signs of this have been found on his remains, and his periods of health followed by periods of illness can be put down to the tendency of TB's symptoms to fluctuate over time, so that in the days before antibiotics patients who went on to die of the disease sometimes enjoyed long periods with few or no symptoms. Whatever it was that ailed Cuthbert claimed the saint in the spring of 687, when he was still in his early fifties.

Godric's sense that he had in some way made contact with Saint Cuthbert during at least one of his visits to Inner Farne spurred him on to even greater religious devotion, and convinced him that he should continue to go on pilgrimages further afield than the North Sea coast of England. He visited Canterbury (though this was long before the martyrdom of Thomas Becket), and the shrine of Saint James at Compostela in Spain. He also visited Rome, the shrine of Saint Giles in Provence, and even the Holy Land. As he roamed the world in this way, was Godric already planning that the end of his wanderings would be in a hermitage like his beloved Cuthbert's?

On one occasion Godric was discussing plans for an imminent pilgrimage with his parents, and seeking their blessing. His mother, who was by then perhaps approaching sixty, expressed her desire to accompany her son, and the two set off for Rome, the old lady shedding her shoes at London and walking barefoot to the city of Saint Peter. At times, when she was tired, or they had to ford a deep river, the sturdy Godric carried his mother on his shoulders.

For part of their pilgrimage, mother and son were accompanied by a mysterious young woman of unimaginable beauty. This lady served the pair, washed Godric's feet and even slept alongside him, though it seems that her relationship with the rugged Englishman remained strictly platonic. Only Godric and his mother could see this radiant creature, though like most pilgrims of the time they were travelling in a large group for safety's sake. When she finally parted from them, just outside London, the lady's farewell speech suggested that she may have been an angel from heaven, who would now return to her father's house, 'a haven of peace'.

The angel-in-disguise story, as related by Godric, seems as baffling and insubstantial as the strangest dream. Was the lady a helping hand from God or, as Godric himself suspected, a temptation, or a bit of both? The reader is tempted not to question the point or authenticity of the tale, but merely to enjoy its charm and ambiguity. Another story about Godric, which has him playing a small but crucial role in the epic drama of world events, may also be a mere will-o'-the-wisp, but if it is true, it gives the future hermit's life a whole new dimension of significance.

The King of Jerusalem

The year 1099 is arguably much more significant in terms of world history than the similar-looking 1066. That was when the First Crusade ended with the capture of the great prize, the holy city of Jerusalem. The Crusade was perhaps the biggest phenomenon to affect Europe and the Middle East during Godric's life; and it seems that the Englishman may have got caught up in a very important event that was part of the long aftermath of the founding of the Crusader State of Jerusalem.

The story of the First Crusade reveals a lot about the politics and religious affiliations that dominated the twelfth century, a century of which our long-lived saint saw an awful lot. For Godric's generation, the known world was arranged in a way that was quite different from what we are used to today. As well as laying bare the world in which Godric's generation lived, the story of the First Crusade reveals something that is usually very elusive to historians: what people living in a distant time knew, or thought they knew, how they thought and felt, and what motivated them. According to some commentators, the First Crusade revealed that many of Godric's contemporaries knew very little, misunderstood a great deal, and were motivated by a tragic combination of fear, ignorance, prejudice and misplaced loyalty.

In 1095, when Godric may still have been under thirty years of age, the Byzantine emperor Alexius I Comnenos sent ambassadors to Pope Urban II in Italy, asking for military help against the Seljuq Turks, who were pressing against the eastern border of his empire and had already swallowed up much of Anatolia. As we shall see, the emperor had also had to contend with threats from his fellow-Christians in the West.

Alexius's empire, which then consisted of little more than the area taken up by modern Greece, was the last remaining fragment of the Roman Empire. It was centred on a famous city on the Bosphorus that has had many names: Byzantium, New Rome, Constantinople and Istanbul. Alexius's capital would eventually be overwhelmed by the Ottoman Turks in 1453, but in 1095 it could still look forward to over three and a half more centuries as the centre of the remaining eastern, Greek-speaking portion of the old empire.

At its height under the sixth-century emperor Justinian the Great, the Byzantine empire had included the whole of Anatolia, many Mediterranean islands, Egypt, and large areas of the Mediterranean coast of Africa; as well as Greece, Italy, the Holy Land, and even part of southern Spain.

By asking the Pope for help Alexius was in effect asking one enemy to assist him in his fight against another. Since the Great Schism of 1054, the Orthodox Church of the Greek-speaking East had regarded itself as separate from the Latin Church of the West, with its capital in Rome (at least some of the time) and its succession of popes and anti-popes. It is likely that Alexius, in his more optimistic moments, expected to be sent a few thousand troops from the West to help him against the Turks, in response to the ambassadors he had sent in 1095. In the event, the Pope's response provoked a hostile, chaotic mass-migration of soldiers and non-combatants.

Pope Urban launched the First Crusade with a powerful speech delivered at Clermont in France in November 1095. There are several surviving accounts of what his holiness actually said on that occasion, but the gist of it seems to have been that Christianity in the East was in peril, and that the Western or Latin Christians should stop warring among themselves and march east as a united army of liberation. What was at stake was not only the Byzantine Empire. Jerusalem itself had already been lost to Christianity. King David's city was then regarded as the centre or navel of the world, and was often placed like a bull's eye in the centre of medieval world maps such as the Mappa Mundi, still to be seen in Hereford Cathedral.

Urban was keen to maintain friendly relations with the Orthodox believers in Alexius's empire, and when he spoke about Christians warring against Christians he may have been thinking of such events as the invasion of what is now Durrës in Albania by the Normans in the summer of 1081. This area, to the north-west of modern Greece, was then in the hands of the Byzantines. The Mediterranean branch of the Norman race that carried out this invasion already controlled Sicily and much of Italy. After the Norman Robert Guiscard had defeated Alexius at Durrës, the invaders went on to make inroads into Greece itself. Although Alexius continued to regard the Normans with the deepest suspicion (and the feeling was certainly mutual) many of them joined the First Crusade.

If the earliest accounts are to be believed, Pope Urban did not hesitate to mix his calls for mutual respect among Christians with an attempt to stir up hatred of the Turks, in his rabble-rousing speech at Clermont. These people, he said, were forcibly circumcising Christian men, and smearing their blood on Christian altars. They were a 'vile race' of 'pagans', 'despised and base', who worshipped demons.

The response to Pope Urban's call for a Crusade against the Turks was overwhelming. Many of the Crusaders who rallied to the cause were more interested in the fact that the Turks controlled the Holy Land than that they were getting dangerously close to Constantinople, far to the north-west. The idea of re-gaining Jerusalem in particular for Christianity had an appeal for some Latin Christians, particularly in France and Germany, that caused them to abandon all rational thought.

Then as now, the city of Jerusalem was sacred to three religions: Judaism, Christianity and Islam. The New Testament states that although Jesus was not born in Jerusalem, his parents went there to offer two doves at the city's celebrated Temple, as was customary for Jewish parents who had just welcomed a new son into the world (see Luke 2:24). It was also here that Jesus 'confounded the elders' during a Passover visit to the city with his parents when he was only twelve years old. Later Jesus taught at the Temple, prophesied about the future of Jerusalem, and overturned the tables of the money-changers. It was also at Jerusalem that the Last Supper and the trial of Jesus took place.

A particular focus for Christian devotion was the Church of the Holy Sepulchre at Jerusalem, regarded as the site of Calvary, where Jesus was crucified, and also of the tomb where Jesus' body lay for three days until his resurrection.

Even in the twelfth century, when travel was slow, difficult and dangerous, Jerusalem attracted Christian pilgrims from Britain and other places in the far north-west of Europe. One motivation for the thousands who joined the First Crusade was that if the Holy City was in Christian hands, in theory European pilgrims would find it easier to get there, and would be better-treated when they arrived. And the Crusade itself was a kind of pilgrimage that, like a peaceful pilgrimage to a holy place in normal times, offered spiritual benefits. Pope Urban asserted that Christian soldiers who marched east would be granted a plenary indulgence; meaning, in effect, that their sins up to that point would be wiped clean, and that they could start again with that longed-for treasure of the guilt-ridden – a clean slate.

The indulgences that the Catholic Church granted in return for repentance, acts of service and even financial contributions were a major bone of contention for Martin Luther and the Protestants. As Christopher Tyerman implied in the introduction to his useful book *Chronicles of the First Crusade*, the Reformation contributed to the decline of the Crusader phenomenon.

One of the most striking characters to arise during the First Crusade was Peter the Hermit, a priest from Amiens in France. Whether he was a genuine hermit, or merely a man with the French name Pierre l'Ermite is unclear. It is possible, of course, that he was a hermit with the name l'Ermite: there are, after all, carpenters called Carpenter and farmers called Farmer. Peter the Hermit was also known as Little Peter, Peter of Amiens and Cucupeter (meaning Peter of the Cowl). If he was or had been a hermit, then that is something he shared with Godric. Like Godric, he may also have lived to a great old age.

Anna Comnena, the daughter of the Byzantine emperor Alexius Comnenus, wrote in her *Alexiad*, a biography of her imperial father, that Cucupeter had been frustrated in his attempt to make a solitary pilgrimage to Jerusalem, and had been mistreated by the local Muslims. Anna calls these people 'Hagarenes' after their supposed biblical matriarch, Hagar, the Egyptian slave of Abraham's wife Sarah. The Byzantine princess also called the Turks 'Ishmaelites' after Abraham's son by Hagar, and accused them of drunkenness, sexual promiscuity and idolatry.

Still sore from his disappointed pilgrimage and his treatment at the hands of the 'Ishmaelites', Cucupeter preached the First Crusade with great energy, and ended up riding a donkey, leading a chaotic host of fanatical followers whose movement is known to historians as the 'People's Crusade'. 'The sight of them' wrote Anna, 'was like many rivers streaming from all sides' (trans. E.A.S. Dawes, 1928).

As it flowed east along the Rhine, this ominous torrent of humanity began to show its true nature when it started to massacre Jews in the settlements through which it passed. Thousands of French and German people were killed in these so-called Rhineland Massacres, which are remembered by the Jews themselves as the Gzerot Tatnó or Edicts of 4856. Others committed suicide or were forced to convert to Christianity. Because of the well-known Crusader antipathy to the Jews, many fled with their Muslim neighbours when their towns and villages in the Middle East were threatened by the westerners at the end of the eleventh century and the beginning of the twelfth.

The Jews of Jerusalem fared even worse that those of the Rhineland when the Crusaders took the city in the summer of 1099. The Muslim rulers of the city had already expelled the Christians who lived there, which allowed the brave Crusaders to massacre almost everyone inside the walls – men, women and children, including many whom they had promised to spare. The Jews of Jerusalem fled to their synagogue, which was burned down while they were all still inside it.

The French chronicler Robert the Monk's account of the carnage at Jerusalem includes apocalyptic scenes of corpses and parts of corpses floating in human blood. The surviving Muslims were forced to drag thousands of their dead fellow-citizens out of the city and pile them up ready for incineration.

The Crusader army that reached Jerusalem in 1099 was a tattered remnant of the huge hosts that had set out from Europe years earlier. Most of the participants in the People's Crusade led by Peter the Hermit had been massacred or enslaved at the Battle of Civetot, fought against the Turks, in 1096. The ranks of those who had joined the more professional Princes' Crusade had been thinned out by enemy action along the way, and by disease, starvation, thirst, exposure and sun-stroke. Others had turned back in disillusionment, having become convinced that the Crusader cause was hopeless. Some, such as Baldwin of Boulogne, who may have had a fateful meeting with Godric of Finchale, had turned aside from the main stream of the Crusaders in search of personal gain.

Tormented by heat and thirst, harassed by enemy attacks and fearful that a large Muslim force might soon arrive to raise their siege, the Crusaders who besieged the city in 1099 managed to breach the walls of Jerusalem with the use of tall siege towers, and mangonels – giant stone-throwing catapults. The Muslim defenders threw everything they had against the towers, including Greek fire, the early medieval equivalent of napalm, but to no avail.

One of the masterminds of the siege was the French aristocrat Godfrey of Bouillon, who was later elected ruler or *princeps* of Jerusalem (he preferred not to call himself 'king'). Robert the Monk shows Godfrey playing a leading role in the siege of 1099, alongside his landless younger brother, Baldwin of Boulogne. In fact Baldwin was not at the siege at all: in the previous year, he had captured the ancient city of Edessa (now Urfa in south-east Turkey) and he was presumably enjoying his new possession, over four hundred miles to the north-east, while Godfrey and his comrades were besieging the Holy City.

Edessa was an Armenian stronghold, and to firm up his title to the city, Baldwin had married Arda, the daughter of Thoros, an Armenian lord. He had previously been married to a Norman lady called Godehilde of Tosny, who accompanied him on the First Crusade, but she had died in 1097. Later, Baldwin would attempt to extricate himself from his marriage to Arda, perhaps partly because her father had not paid all of the dowry he had promised his new French son-in-law.

When his older brother Godfrey died, perhaps of typhoid, in 1100, Baldwin quickly made himself ruler of Jerusalem, and, unlike his brother, had no hesitation in calling himself king of the place. Baldwin understood the value of looking like a king, which was easier for him than it was for many because he stood a head taller than most of his contemporaries. He was fit and strong and wore a long, black beard. As the Victorian writer Walter Besant wrote in his 1871 history of Jerusalem, Baldwin 'was fond of personal splendour and display. When he rode out in the town of Edessa a golden buckler, with the device of an eagle, was borne before him, and two horsemen rode in front blowing trumpets'.

Although he evidently felt he could afford such a show, Baldwin was often short of money. In the spring of 1101, when he heard that a wealthy Arab tribe was passing through Transjordan, he led a detachment of his army to attack them at night, kill all the men, capture the women and children and seize all their valuables. When he heard that one of the women was going into labour, Baldwin set her and her servant free and made sure they had camels, food, drink, shelter and slaves. The lady, the wife of a sheikh, was safely delivered of a child and was soon discovered in her tent by her husband. The grateful sheikh hurried after Baldwin and assured him that he would not forget his kindness.

The ambitions of the Egyptians were among the most serious threats to Baldwin's kingdom. They had an impressive navy, and when their advancing army reached Ramla, some twenty miles to the north-west of Jerusalem, in May 1102, the new king of the Holy City felt that he should respond. Unfortunately Baldwin's information was faulty, and he believed that he would have to deal with nothing more than a small party of Egyptian raiders.

With an inadequate force of about five hundred horsemen, Baldwin rode out to meet a mighty host of invading Egyptians. The Frankish force was quickly overwhelmed and Baldwin was forced to take refuge, with a few other survivors, in Ramla itself. The situation was desperate. As night fell, the Franks found themselves cooped up in a tiny tower, surrounded by Egyptians. It was then that a local Arab dignitary turned up and begged an audience with the king. He was the sheikh whose wife Baldwin had helped when she was in labour, after his brutal raid on the Arab tribe. The sheikh warned the king that the Egyptians were preparing a dawn raid, and offered him a way to escape. With just four companions, Baldwin slipped away on his fine horse, Gazelle.

Besant was inclined to think that the tale of the grateful sheikh was a little too good to be true, and mentioned that there was only one source for it. The source is, however, William of Tyre, regarded as one of the best chroniclers of the period. Since William began to write his Latin *Historia* almost seventy years after these events (around the time Saint Godric died), and over fifty years after the death of Baldwin himself, it may be that he was merely setting down a legend that had grown up in the interim.

As dawn broke over Ramla the Egyptians piled faggots around the base of the tower and set light to them. The Franks made a desperate attempt to break out, but many were only rewarded with the satisfaction of dying in battle rather than perishing as a result of smoke-inhalation. Others were captured and sold as slaves in Egypt.

The Egyptians knew that Baldwin had evaded them, and they scoured the countryside around Ramla in a vain attempt to find him. For two days, the king's party was obliged to hide in the foothills north of Ramla, until it seemed safe to ride for the coast at Arsuf. It was here that the future hermit of Finchale, then in his mid-thirties, may have been the English 'pirate' who conveyed the king to the port city of Jaffa. This character is mentioned by the chronicler Albert of Aix: the fact that Godric is thought to have been on a pilgrimage to Jerusalem at the time makes it more likely that this Godric really was our Godric.

Baldwin's Armenian wife Arda was then at Jaffa with much of her husband's court. Garbled reports of the massacres at Ramla reached them, and it was assumed that the King of Jerusalem was dead. This impression was reinforced when Egyptian ships began to appear in the harbour, and a soldier on board one of them held up a severed head that looked a lot like Baldwin's. In fact, it was the head of one Gerbod of Winthinc, who merely resembled the king. Just when all seemed hopeless, Baldwin's standard was spotted on a small ship approaching from the north. This was the craft belonging to Godric the English pirate, and it was agile enough to land Baldwin before the larger ships of the Egyptian fleet could stop it. From Jaffa the lucky king was able to return to Jerusalem and put together a new army.

Nineteenth-century statue of Godric on St Godric's RC church, Durham

Norman font at St Giles's, Durham

Statue of Giles on St Giles's church, Durham

The River Wear at Finchale

Ruins of the Prior's house

Hidden column emerging from a newer wall

Godric's grave at Finchale

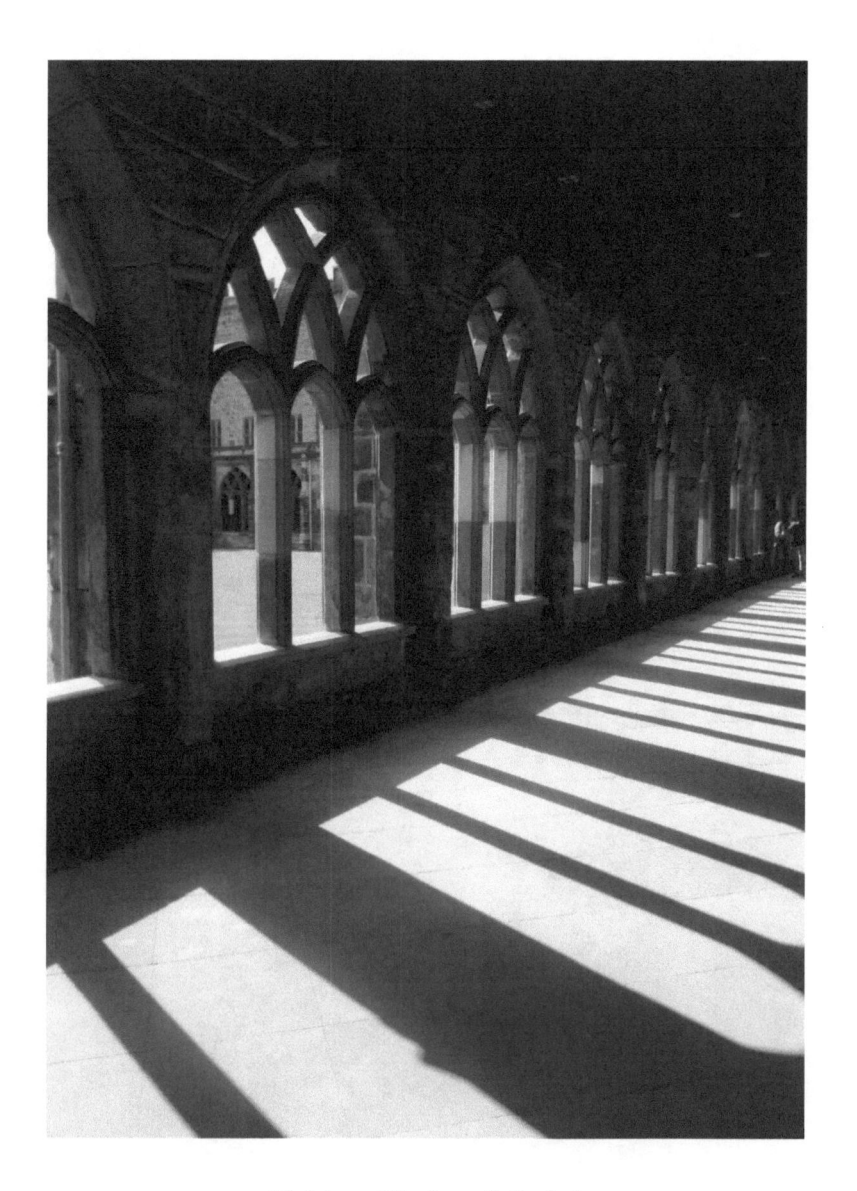

Cloisters at Durham Cathedral

Godric from British Library MS Cotton Faustina B VI, vol. II (1425)

The Road to Finchale

After his time as a sea-captain, saviour of King Baldwin and perhaps pirate were behind him, Godric spent a while wandering alone through England, sleeping rough. Rice calls his chapter on this part of the saint's life 'Godric the Tramp', though it is clear that unlike many modern homeless people, Godric embraced this way of life willingly.

An attempt to start again in a fresh town where he thought he would be unknown proved abortive, when Godric was recognised by some relatives at Carlisle. This would have been more likely in those days, when the population of the whole of England was so much smaller. At around two million, it would have been equivalent to well under a third of the current population of London alone.

Godric retreated to the woods, where he 'camped out' as we would now say, living on berries and nuts, and making friends with the woodland creatures. After this, 'God's tramp', as Rice calls him, took to wandering again. By this time, Godric had acquired his book of psalms, which Robert Hegge claimed he hung from his little finger until the finger itself became deformed.

Chance, or providence, brought Godric to Wolsingham. This Weardale town is about fourteen miles to the west of Durham City, and Reginald's mention of it is its first appearance in the pages of history. Today, visitors see a picturesque County Durham market-town on the River Wear, but the main attraction for Godric was the home of an elderly hermit, Aelric, who lived deep in the forest in a rough hut that he had built himself.

Aelric had lived with the Benedictine monks at Durham, but Francis Rice suggests that he may never have been a monk himself, as he was virtually illiterate. He had embraced the hermit's way of life, and was therefore fairly close to Saint Benedict's idea of a Christian hermit, as set out in his influential Rule. This celebrated book of monastic advice and regulations was already over six hundred years old when Godric came to live with Aelric. Close to the start of his very first chapter, Benedict implies that the only legitimate hermits and anchorites are people who have lived a long time in a monastic community, and wish to spend their last years as hermits. Their long experience of life in the cloister has allowed them to build up their spiritual defences, and they are now ready to wage solitary warfare against 'the vices of the body and the mind' (trans. Parry, 1990).

Here Benedict makes it clear that Christian hermits should definitely be 'proper' monks, first and foremost, which would seem to exclude Aelric to some extent. Benedict has nothing good to say about people who live as monks and hermits but who have never subjected themselves to any kind of monastic rule. These people Benedict calls 'sarabaites': they lie to God by appearing to be monks, but in fact 'their law consists in yielding to their desires'. Worse than the sarabaites are the gyrovagues, another species of false monk. Gyrovagues wander around, living on the hospitality offered by genuine monastic communities, and falling into the sin of gluttony.

It must be said that during certain phases of his life, Godric got close to living as a sarabaite or a gyrovague, and in fact he never seems to have lived in a cloister as a novice, let alone a fully-fledged monk. He made his own way, which in the long run proved to be acceptable to the Durham Benedictines; but Saint Benedict himself may have treated a man like Godric with a great deal of suspicion.

Godric stayed for two years with Aelric, and though their dense forest habitat was supposed to be infested with dangerous wolves, they lived in harmony with their canine neighbours. Soon, however, the senior hermit's health began to fail, and Godric became his devoted nurse. When Aelric died, his younger companion saw his soul rising from his body, as Saint Cuthbert had seen the soul of Aidan ascending to heaven so many centuries before. Soon Godric was also blessed with a vision of Saint Cuthbert himself, who appeared to him and instructed him to go on one last pilgrimage, to the Holy Land. After that, said Cuthbert, Godric must find a place called Finchale, and make a new hermitage for himself there.

In 1894, the Palestine Pilgrimage Text Society published a selection from anonymous accounts of pilgrimages to the Holy Land, translated into English by Aubrey Stewart. All of these were from the eleventh or twelfth centuries, and it is clear that for some of the pilgrims included, their pilgrimage was to do with something other than just religion. One pilgrim seems to have been far too interested in spotting attractive women and sampling good food in the countries he passed through, and another gives a detailed and critical account of the various Christian groups to be found in the Holy Land, but from the military point of view. In his opinion the Syrian Christians, for instance, 'are useless in war'.

It is likely that both of Godric's pilgrimages to the Holy Land happened after Jerusalem had been captured by the Crusaders in 1099. In theory, the new Christian hegemony there should have made life easier for Christian pilgrims, but in practice a journey such as Godric was now attempting for the second time could not but be arduous and dangerous. Like the First Crusaders, many pilgrims perished *en route*, either from hunger, sickness or exhaustion, and many were attacked by highwaymen or pirates. Many pilgrim ships were dangerously overcrowded, and liable to become very unhealthy, or to capsize. On his second and last pilgrimage to the Holy Land, our future saint made things even more difficult for himself by eating only stale barley bread, and then only when he was actually fainting with hunger.

Godric carried nothing more than a staff and a small bag or 'scrip', and slept, either inside or in the open air, with no covering or other bedding. When he slept in one of the hostels that were scattered along the pilgrim routes, he would remove any mattress or blankets and sleep uncovered on the bare wood of the bed. His clothing was inadequate and uncomfortable, and included one of the hair-shirts that seem to have been regarded as an indispensable item by generations of Christian saints. Godric's attire may have become even less inhabitable during the long months of his journey, as Reginald implies that he did not wash either his clothes or himself until he reached the River Jordan.

Remembering, perhaps, that his mother had travelled from London to Rome and back barefoot, Godric decided to go one better (or worse) and donned a pair of shoes, made of reeds, that were actually less comfortable than no shoes at all. These he abandoned when he reached the Jordan, and thereafter went barefoot for the rest of his life, even in the snow, ice and mud of Finchale. On one of the rare occasions when Godric left Finchale once he had got there, he walked barefoot over ice into Durham. The skin of the soles of his feet stuck to the ice and tore off as he walked, leaving a trail of bloody footsteps.

A pilgrimage to the Holy Land, particularly to Jerusalem itself, is still an aspiration for many Jews, Christians, Muslims and others. The chronic political instability of the area puts many people off, as well as the expense of the journey. People with doubts about how the modern state of Israel is run may also hesitate to appear to support the young nation by visiting it.

In the twelfth century, pious visitors to the Holy Land were shown sites that seemed calculated to instil in them a sense that the events and characters to be found in the Bible really did happen, and in specific places that could still be identified. Some of the tales attached to these people and places cannot be found in the Old or New Testaments at all, but can be traced to local traditions, apocryphal works or other texts that were written after the books of the Bible as we know it.

Some of these tales fill gaps in, or answer questions raised by, the biblical narrative, in ways that can seem a little too convenient. What did Jesus do during the three days between his crucifixion and resurrection? According to the apocryphal *Acts of Pilate*, he descended into hell and challenged Satan's dominion. This was the Harrowing of Hell, featured in many medieval paintings, and alluded to by, among others, Dante and the authors of the English medieval mystery plays. Another question was, didn't the Roman authorities keep some kind of record of the crucifixion? Of course – this can also be found in the *Acts of Pilate*.

What happened to the Star of Bethlehem after it had done its job of leading the Magi to Bethlehem? It disappeared into a well at Bethlehem, which was shown to pilgrims. Bethlehem was also the birthplace of King David, the place to go to see the tomb of Rachel, the Old Testament matriarch, and the location of the place where the scholar-saint Jerome lived for many years. Jerome lived in the same cave where Jesus was said to have been born.

The legend-makers of the early Christian centuries also tackled the question of what happened to the True Cross after it had been used for Jesus' crucifixion. It lay buried for centuries until it was discovered by Saint Helena, the mother of the Roman emperor Constantine, in the year 334. How did she know that she had found the True Cross? A leper touched it, and was healed. In Godric's time, pilgrims visited the spot where Helena's discovery is supposed to have been made, and also the place where the tree from which the Cross was originally fashioned was cut down.

As well as visiting or re-visiting some or all of the pilgrim sites in and around Jerusalem on his second visit, Godric made special visits to various hermits in the area, and volunteered to help out at the Hospital of Saint John the Baptist in Jerusalem itself. Perhaps his experience of nursing the Wolsingham hermit Aelric through his last illness persuaded him that he might have something to offer in this field.

Some remains of Godric's Jerusalem hospital were rediscovered in 2013, when the area was being surveyed in preparation for the building of a new restaurant. Archaeologists found the ruins of a large, high-ceilinged hall with pointed stone arches, and smaller rooms leading off it. This was part of a remarkable institution which, at its height, could take as many as two thousand patients. Some of these were brought in on camels or horses – a medieval ambulance service – and there are signs that the hall discovered in 2013 was used for stabling these animals. Explorers also found evidence of a smithy here.

Contemporary accounts reveal that at Saint John's Hospital there were different wards for patients with different conditions, as in a modern hospital. There were also separate areas for men and women, and an orphanage for children who had begun life as abandoned babies. To the European 'hospitallers' who ran the place, much of this would have seemed innovative, but some of these ideas had been well-known in the Muslim world for a while. Saint John's Hospital is said to have benefited enormously from the expertise of local Muslim physicians, some of whom were far in advance of any doctors in the west.

The eleventh-century Persian polymath Ibn Sina, known to Europeans as Avicenna, wrote a work called the Qanun fi'l-tibb, or *Canon of Medicine* which remained a standard textbook in both

East and West for five hundred years. The Qanun has information on nearly eight hundred drugs, including cannabis and opium. There are also detailed descriptions of cataracts, diabetes, pleurisy and tuberculosis, and accounts of operations for the removal of kidney stones and haemorrhoids. Avicenna also knew how diseases like tuberculosis could spread (though not why), and that soil and water could harbour disease.

Not all of the Muslim medics Godric may have worked with in Jerusalem would have been Avicennas, but they were enlightened in that they would treat Jews, Christians and Muslims. They would also have been of great benefit to their European colleagues because they knew how to tackle local afflictions, unknown in Europe, under local conditions, using materials that were locally available.

Despite the efforts of the medical staff, the hospital lost around fifty of its patients (perhaps two and a half percent) every twenty-four hours, according to the twelfth century German priest and pilgrim John of Wurzburg. Given the location of the hospital, many of these patients probably succumbed to fevers of one kind or another, and Godric must have known that by venturing into the fever wards he would have been running a considerable risk.

The 'hospitallers' who were responsible for the hospital eventually developed a military arm, known as the Knights Hospitallers.

Did Godric gain useful knowledge about diseases and treatments at his Jerusalem hospital, that he was able to apply during his later life back in England? It is surely significant that while he was living in what is now County Durham, he worked in a church attached to a hospital, and showed a particular devotion to John the Baptist, to whom the Jerusalem hospital was dedicated.

Godric never went back to the Holy Land: in fact as far as we know he never left England after he had returned from his last pilgrimage. Although his body never strayed very far any more, he was able to travel in the spirit, and could see remote places like Jerusalem without stirring from his native country. He took an interest in how Jerusalem in particular had changed since he had lived there.

The hermit's miraculous ability to see straight through the horizon is reminiscent of the Old Testament book of Ezekiel. In chapter eight of that book we learn that the spirit of the prophet, whose body remained in what is now Iraq, was swept up and taken to Jerusalem, where he was able to observe what was happening to the city and its temple. This must have felt something like the experience of being in some types of 'immersive' video game, where the players feel that they have indeed been transported to, say, an imaginary planet, when in fact they are just sitting at a computer at home. A similar experience might be had by tuning in to a webcam set up in a street in, say, Tokyo, and seeing what is happening there in real time, when one is actually thousands of miles away.

St Giles and St Mary

Around 1112, when he was probably in his late forties, Godric became a doorkeeper at St Giles's church outside Durham, then a very new church, built by Bishop Ranulf Flambard as part of a complex that included a so-called 'hospital'. This was not a hospital in the modern sense, or like the Hospital of Saint John that Godric had known in Jerusalem: it was really an almshouse – a place where the old and infirm could live when they could no longer support themselves by their labour, and when friends and relatives could not or would not help.

With close observation and a little imagination, visitors can see that Flambard's church, which still stands, was originally much smaller than it is now. Over the centuries, the place has become taller, longer, and lighter, larger windows having been cut out of some of the walls.

Modern visitors to Giles's, a warm and welcoming church, are shown a wall with high, small, round-arched windows which is part of the original Norman building. They are also shown the old stone font, which looks so heavy and solid that one suspects that it would survive intact even if the rest of the church were swept away by a tornado. As doorkeeper, a very lowly type of cleric,

Giles would no doubt have been familiar with the Norman door that still survives here: these days it is sheltered from the elements, having long ago become the inner door of the church's porch.

Godric would have been responsible for unlocking this and other doors for services, then locking them again when the church was empty. He would also have acted as a sort of janitor, responsible for sweeping up inside and out. Always good with his hands, the future hermit would have been the ideal man to fix leaks and cracks, and to generally nurse St Giles's through the inevitable teething-troubles that come with a new building. The role of doorkeeper was seen as a preliminary step before training for the priesthood, but Godric's plans were not to take him in that direction.

As a fit, healthy middle-aged bachelor, the newcomer to Durham might have become a person of interest for many unmarried women and widows, and their match-making friends and relatives. Godric might have found himself at the head of a ready-made family, complete with step-children and step-grandchildren, and the prospect of children of his own, but if any of the city's lonely ladies set their caps at the Norfolk man, nothing seems to have come of it.

Godric could not have become a doorkeeper at St Giles's if Bishop Ranulf Flambard had not built the place in 1112. Likewise, he may have found it more difficult to set himself up as a hermit at Finchale if Flambard had not given him permission to do so. From Godric's point of view, this particular bishop of Durham must have looked like a saint; but others would not have characterised him in that way.

Flambard's chequered career demonstrates a lot about how the Normans ran England at this time. The bishop was himself a Norman, born around 1060, the son of a humble parish priest from the Bessin, a part of Normandy that includes the town of Bayeux.

His mother is supposed to have been a sorceress, of all things. Her son soon shook off his modest origins, and by his mid-twenties he was working high up in William the Conqueror's government. He even appears in the Domesday book as a landowner, with properties bringing in perhaps tens of thousands of pounds a year, at today's values.

Flambard really began to thrive under the Conqueror's successor, William Rufus, for whom he became a very important official, with power over crucial matters concerning the church, the law and finance. He was therefore an example of the way that men in holy orders, with their superior literacy, ran all sorts of things in those days.

One might expect that churchmen working as, in effect, civil servants, politicians and judges, as Flambard was, might be influenced by the example of Jesus, and do their jobs in an entirely blameless and ethical way. But Flambard, who scored very low in piety, seems not to have asked 'what would Jesus do?' when faced with important decisions. His chief skill was as a royal 'exactor', charged with extracting the maximum amount of wealth from England for the benefit of the king, and himself. Laws relating to taxation and other matters were twisted and exploited to the utmost, so that when Bishop William de St-Calais of Durham died in 1096, Ranulf Flambard was able to pay the king the huge sum of a thousand pounds to buy himself the bishopric of Durham.

In August 1100 William Rufus was killed during a hunting expedition in the New Forest. An arrow pierced his lung, and ever since scholars have been debating whether his death was an accident or an assassination. Ranulf Flambard, who had enjoyed a meteoric rise during the late king's reign, now found himself out of favour. Less than a fortnight after King William's death, the new king, Henry I, had the bishop of Durham locked up in the Tower of London. Six months later, Flambard escaped. His escape has been described as 'pure Gilbert and Sullivan'.

Somebody smuggled a rope to Ranulf in a jug of wine. The bishop got his guards drunk on the wine and climbed down the rope to freedom. He sought shelter in his native Normandy with Robert Curthose, the new king's brother. This shows how the Norman dynasty that now ruled England continued to maintain their dukedom across the Channel: the problem was that Normandy was sometimes controlled by enemies of the English king.

Although Flambard assisted Robert Curthose in his unsuccessful attempt to invade England in 1101, King Henry evidently felt that the exiled bishop should be allowed to come back to England, and in 1106 Ranulf returned to his see. As well as building his hospital and St Giles's church, he built the predecessor of Framwellgate Bridge over the River Wear at Durham, improved Durham's city walls and continued the building of the cathedral, which had been started by his predecessor, Bishop William de St-Calais.

These all seem very worthwhile projects, but the way Flambard funded them, and the general manner in which he lived and ran his diocese, attracted the kind of criticism that had dogged him throughout his career. He filled many offices with his relatives, including sons who may or may not have also been the sons of a wife or various mistresses.

Flambard certainly had a Saxon wife or mistress, a lady called Aelfgifu, who lived at Huntingdon. On one of his visits there, he took a fancy to her beautiful niece Theodora. The girl was exceptionally pious and had decided to remain celibate and unmarried at all costs. Probably under twenty herself at the time, she was certainly not keen to have extra-marital sex with a bishop in his mid-fifties. As Flambard pressed himself on her, she pretended to be enthusiastic about the prospect, and suggested that she lock the door. She did so, but with herself on the outside and her would-be seducer trapped within. Later, Theodora changed her name to Christina, and is now remembered as Christina of Markyate (in Hertfordshire), a prioress and the subject of a remarkable biography.

Flambard funded work on Durham Cathedral out of monies that should have gone to the local monks, and in the late summer of 1128 the ailing bishop was carried into the half-built church to make a public confession of his wrong-doing and to formally restore these monies to the monks. A month later, he died.

While he was connected to St Giles' church, it is unlikely that Godric could have failed to hear about the church's saint, Giles himself, especially on the feast of Saint Giles, which is held on the first of September. It may be that stories of this French saint reinforced Godric's determination embrace the life of a hermit.

Giles is a rather misty, semi-legendary figure: it is not even clear exactly when he lived or where he came from, although he is associated with Saint-Gilles in the south of France, a place which Godric is supposed to have visited as a pilgrim. Giles may have lived in the sixth century, and some say that he was actually a noble Athenian by birth, who had come to live in France.

The nineteenth-century statue of Giles that stands above the north door of St Giles's in Durham shows him with a deer at his feet. According to the *Golden Legend*, a wildly popular set of saints' lives from the thirteenth century, God sent this animal to feed Giles with her milk, once he had become a hermit. When the deer was threatened by hunters, the saint protected her, and was injured by one of the hunters' arrows.

In the words of William Caxton's fifteenth-century English translation of the *Golden Legend*, the saint and the deer hid in a bush that was 'so thick that no man ne beast might enter therein for the brambles and thorns that were there'. Parts of Godric's habitat at Finchale would certainly have answered to this description, and still do today. As we shall see, Godric is also supposed to have protected a deer from hunters and, like Giles, he grew his own food, though Caxton's *Legend* attributes Giles's crops to a miracle rather than hard work. According to Caxton, it was 'by his merits' that Giles 'chased away the sterility and barrenness that was in that country, and caused great plenty of goods'.

The *Golden Legend* tells us that Giles lived in a pit of some kind: this reminds us of Godric's little house by the Wear, which was essentially a roofed-in hole. Like Godric, Giles was befriended by the great and the good, though unlike Godric Giles was persuaded by a local king to found a monastery and become a bishop.

Godric may have gone on his pilgrimage to Giles's shrine in France as a penance for sins with which he had become entangled during an unexpected period of his life, when he worked as a steward or 'reeve' in the house of some great man. Why an old sea-dog like Godric would have thought of embracing such an existence is a mystery: in any case, it turned out that it did not suit him at all. He discovered that other servants of the owner of the great house were systematically stealing from him and that, worse, they were exploiting the great man's tenants.

To his horror, Godric discovered that he had been eating food exacted unjustly from the local peasants. When he broke the news to his master, the man claimed that he did not care, and that the matter was of no importance. If Godric's master had been a Norman noble whose henchmen were exploiting the local Saxons, Godric's sense of the nastiness of it all may have been particularly intense. He washed his hands of the whole business, and left his master's service.

After a short time as door-keeper there, Godric left St Giles's in Durham and attached himself to St Mary le Bow church, on the city's peninsula and in the shadow of Durham Cathedral, which was then a vast, busy, dusty building-site. Most of what visitors see of St Mary's today dates from the seventeenth century or later. An older church on this site collapsed in 1637. The name of the church is supposed to derive from the fact that it was here that Saint Cuthbert's remains rested when they were first brought to Durham in 995. Housed in the wooden coffin that is still on display among the cathedral's treasures, Cuthbert was sheltered under an improvised 'church of boughs', hence the name St Mary le Bow. Since 1972, the deconsecrated church has been home to the Durham Heritage Museum.

For Godric, the attraction of St Mary's lay in part in its school, where he may soon have been sitting down to lessons, a man in his forties among the young boys. His use of his beloved psalter and his time attending services at Giles's must have given him some idea of Latin: now, close to Cuthbert's shrine, his knowledge of the language was getting a final polish, preliminary to Godric's retreat into the wilderness.

The Hermit's Life

Though stories of Saint Giles might have strengthened Godric's determination to embrace the hermit's life, he may also have known enough Church history to have been inspired by the example of even earlier Christian hermits.

For a while during the fourth century, Saint Anthony of Egypt was accepted as the first of these. That was until some time in the 370s, when Saint Jerome, who, as we know, lived for a time as a hermit at Bethlehem, wrote a little book about Saint Paul of Thebes. By the time Jerome penned his account, Paul had probably been dead for over thirty years. Early in his book on Paul, Jerome apologises that he has found very little information about this saint: he contrasts this with the 'full tradition' that already existed about Anthony.

Despite the scarcity of data, Jerome resists the temptation to include certain wild stories about Paul in the main body of his narrative: for instance that his hair reached down to his heels, and that he lived in a cave underground. In fact Jerome's *Vita Pauli primi eremitae* ('Life of Paul the first hermit') includes little more than an account of two visits paid to Paul of Thebes by Saint Anthony himself, some time in the 340s – and Paul was already dead by the time Anthony made his second visit.

Anthony was alerted to Paul's existence in a dream. He discovered that he lived in a cave in the Theban desert, by a spring and a palm-tree. An Egyptian like Anthony himself, Paul had originally sought out his retreat to avoid the persecution of Christians by the Roman emperors Decius (died 251) and Valerian (d. c. 260).

Sharp-eyed readers may already have noticed that if Valerian died around 260, then Paul must have been a hermit for around eighty years before Anthony came to visit him: Paul was able to fit these long desert decades into his life because, like Godric, he is supposed to have lived for over a century. In fact he lived long enough to outlive the persecution of Christians by the Roman emperors. In 313, when Paul was a mere stripling in his mid-eighties, the emperor Constantine issued his Edict of Milan, ushering in a new age of tolerance for the followers of Jesus. This means that for over twenty years Paul had not needed to stay in the desert to avoid persecution: evidently he remained in his cave for other reasons.

At home in the dark days of the Decian persecution, Paul had felt himself to be particularly liable to be seized by the authorities because of the machinations of his brother-in-law. This charming relative calculated that if he could get his wife's Christian brother killed, he would inherit the family property. During the persecutions of the various emperors, this sort of seedy plotting must have been happening all over the empire. Discontented husbands were no doubt informing on unwanted wives, wives on husbands, and children, perhaps looking for a windfall like Paul's brother-in-law, must have been betraying Christian parents.

The account of Paul's life contained in Jerome's *Vita* resembles Reginald's description of Godric in many respects. Not only did both hermits live to a great age: they both lived near water. While Godric had his iron tunic, Paul had clothing fashioned from the leaves of the palm-tree that grew outside his cave. Paul got much of his food from this tree, which was presumably a date palm. The Egyptians have been growing dates since ancient times.

When Anthony first visited Paul, he found that a wolf was admitted into the older hermit's compound before he was. This suggests that the senior saint was able to make friends with wild animals, just like Godric, who also counted wolves among his associates. Animals are also said to have served Godric and obeyed him, and, according to Jerome, when Anthony found Paul dead and started digging a grave for him, two desert lions dropped in and volunteered to help out.

As he entered middle age, Paul began to get daily rations of bread delivered by birds. In Godric's case, the situation was reversed: he fed the local wildlife on his excess food. Perhaps some of the creatures who benefited from Godric's generosity were the finches after whom Finchale may have been named. Jerome tells us that when Anthony visited Paul, the daily bread-ration was doubled.

Another figure who was fed on bread brought by birds was Elijah, an Old Testament prophet who appears in both books of Kings. Like Paul of Thebes, Elijah fled into the wilderness to avoid persecution. A follower of the Hebrew god, Elijah had angered King Ahab by prophesying three years of drought. This, he told the king, was God's response to his majesty's devotion to a rival deity, Baal.

In many respects, Elijah resembles the later figure of Jesus. He performed miracles, including bringing people back from the dead, and challenged the authorities with his distinctive views. It is hardly surprising that some first-century Jews thought that Jesus *was* Elijah. Like Jesus, Elijah is not supposed to have been buried on earth: he rose bodily into heaven, in his case in a chariot. While many Christians await the second coming of Jesus, Jews put out a cup and leave a door open for Elijah during the Passover feast.

Like Elijah, Jesus also played the hermit when he retired into the wilderness, for forty days and nights.

At the beginning of his account of Paul of Thebes, Jerome dismisses the idea that Elijah could be counted as the first hermit, because he was a prophet, not a monk. This makes little sense, as there is nothing to say that a hermit cannot be a prophet as well, and there were always Christian hermits who were not monks or nuns. To say that Elijah was not a hermit because he was a prophet is like saying that a chair is not a chair because, like a table, it has legs. Certainly Godric the hermit of Finchale had the gift of prophecy.

Jerome's logic also seems to falter when he argues, in the same passage, that John the Baptist cannot be counted as the first hermit because he was a prophet even before he was born. Whatever Jerome thought, certain features of John the Baptist's story are reminiscent of tales of the later Christian hermits. John lived in a remote spot by a river, wore unconventional clothes and ate locusts and wild honey.

In many paintings and statues, John's garments appear to be made out of camel skin, but it is more likely that they were woven out of camel hair. This might have made them itchy and uncomfortable, like the hair shirts worn by many hermits and saints, and like Godric's awkward iron tunic.

The fact that the Baptist prophesied, spoke out against the authorities and was martyred connects him to Elijah and Jesus as well as many later saints. Although John may have lived as a solitary hermit for some of the time, his preaching and his offer of baptism attracted people to his home by the River Jordan. Many later saints attracted crowds of visitors, who cannot always have been welcome.

While Jerome discounts Elijah as a hermit, Athanasius of Alexandria, the author of a biography of Anthony of Egypt, has his saint saying that the Old Testament prophet should serve as a model for Christian saints and hermits. This forms part of a lengthy sermon by Anthony, which stands in the middle of Athanasius's account. While advising his listeners that demons can do them no harm, the Egyptian reveals that he has seen and heard demons, and even Satan himself, in many forms during his long periods of isolation. He has even felt them, when they shook his hermitage with an earthquake. On this occasion, his prayers and his 'unshaken heart' protected him.

In his sermon, Anthony implies that he has learned by long experience to distinguish good spirits from bad ones: he advises that if believers are uncertain, they should boldly ask the apparitions who they are.

The fact that he was visited by both good and bad spirits is something Anthony of Egypt, also known as Anthony the Great, shares with Godric. The Egyptian's early experiences of the hermit's life, as recounted by Athanasius, are, however, different in character to Godric's own. Reading about the Englishman's life by the Wear it is easy to be charmed by the free, open-air nature of it. The same is true of Jerome's account of Paul of Thebes's life, though we should remember that both Paul and Godric would have suffered some punishing extremes of weather.

By contrast, some of Anthony's first experiences of holy isolation were in an underground tomb, and an abandoned fort by the River Nile. He walled himself up in the fort using a barrier of loaves of dried bread. It seems that the sands rose around the walls of the fort, but did not penetrate inside, so that again Anthony found himself, in effect, underground.

Later in life, Anthony grew tired of the constant visitors to his hermitage, and joined a caravan of Arabs that was heading into the deep desert. There he found a mountain with a clear, cold spring at its base, and resolved to stay in its shadow. This was one of the

Red Sea Hills, that run parallel to that sea, which itself divides Egypt from the Sinai peninsula.

Passing Arabs and Christian friends brought provisions to Anthony's mountain fastness, but he yearned for independence and began growing his own food. This is something else that makes Anthony similar to Godric: no doubt his busy new life of planting and watering was healthier for the earlier saint than the periods he had spent walled up in an old tomb and an abandoned fort.

In theory, both Godric and Anthony were at risk from dangerous animals, living in the wild places where they dwelt, but both were able to live in peace with these ferocious creatures, and even to have some influence over them. In Anthony's case, the hermit had more to fear from predators than just their natural fierceness: on nights when the Egyptian prayed right through the hours of darkness, the devil would send animals to attack him. At one point the adversary sent 'almost all the hyenas in that desert' to swarm around the saint, but he calmly stood up to them. He told them that if God had sent them, then he was happy to be eaten alive. If, on the other hand, they had been sent by demons, then they should return to their dens. 'When Anthony said this they fled, driven by that word as with a whip' (trans. Ellershaw, 1892).

Hyenas are usually associated with the African savannahs, and not with the Egyptian desert, but Egypt has its own, distinctive, striped hyenas, which are currently endangered. On one occasion Anthony proved that that characteristic Egyptian animal, the crocodile, was just as harmless to him as a clan of hyenas. Forced to wade through a canal full of the reptiles, he rendered them tame by the power of prayer alone.

In art and legend, Anthony is associated with pigs, though the story of his keeping a pet pig is not mentioned by Athanasius. The saint may have worked as a swine-herd at some point, and there are tales about later monks who followed the Egyptian claiming the runts of the litters, or 'tantony pigs', as their own. Anthony mentions pigs in the sermon, recorded by Athanasius, where he assures his hearers that the devil is not to be feared, because he has no real power to hurt the righteous. Here the Egyptian references the New Testament passage where Jesus allows demons to escape into the bodies of pigs, which then drown themselves (see Matthew 8:31). The episode of the so-called Gadarene swine could not have happened, Anthony insists, unless God had allowed it.

As well as bravely confronting a cackle of hyenas, Anthony was not afraid to take on pagan Greeks who journeyed to his mountain retreat on purpose to challenge his Christian faith. In his *Life* of Anthony, Athanasius often uses the word 'Greeks' as a synonym for 'pagans', and the implication is that although by the middle of the fourth century many of the local Egyptians had converted to Christianity, many of the Greeks who lived in the valley of the Nile continued to revere both Greek and Egyptian gods. In fact the Greeks who ruled Egypt before it became part of the Roman Empire encouraged the worship of Serapis, a god who combined the characteristics of both Greek and Egyptian deities. Today we think of Egypt as a Muslim country, but Anthony died more than two centuries before the birth of Muhammed.

It seems that the pagan Greeks who disputed with Anthony on matters of religion expected to have an easy time of it, because it was widely known that the hermit had had very little education. He could not even understand Greek, though this language was widely spoken in Egypt, was the language of the Septuagint and the New Testament, and was also used as a *lingua franca* throughout the Mediterranean world.

Although Anthony's disputes with the pagan Greeks must have been a little cumbersome, as he was forced to work through an interpreter, the hermit managed to make them slink off with their tails between their legs, just like the hyenas, despite his own lack of learning. He pointed out that the pagan gods committed adultery and even seduced young boys: he was probably thinking of the Greek god Zeus, a serial philanderer who abducted Ganymede, a beautiful youth. Turning to the local pantheon, Anthony mocked the Egyptian habit of worshipping 'senseless animals . . . four-footed beasts, creeping things and the likenesses of men'. Here he was probably referencing ancient deities such as the cat-god Bastet, the jackal Anubis, and the ancient Egyptians' reverence for the dung-beetle. The hermit also objected to the local habit of mummifying the dead, and insisted that dead Christians should be buried, and not preserved in tombs built above the ground.

The fact that the unlettered Anthony could still confound pagan Greeks who mocked his lack of learning conveys the familiar message that the essentials of Christianity are easy to grasp, and that the objections Christians raise vis-a-vis other religions are evident to anybody. The accessibility of the Christian message is one of the more attractive features of the faith. In fact some of the more learned early Christians were taken aback by the simplicity, even the crudeness, of the new message they were trying to embrace.

While Christianity in Egypt still faced challenges from paganism, forms of Christianity that both Anthony and Athanasius regarded as heretical were probably more of a threat. The latter was bishop of the cosmopolitan city of Alexandria, but only intermittently. He was often forced to go into exile when the Arian heresy gained the upper hand. The followers of a Libyan called Arius, the Arians disagreed with Christians like Athanasius about the nature of Jesus. Of course Anthony disagreed with the Arians, described their teachings as poisonous, and even made a journey from his mountain into the city of Alexandria to assert that, despite what they claimed, he was not an Arian, and believed that their ideas were as foolish as those of the pagans.

Since the Arians were Athanasius's enemies, it is tempting to speculate that, in his *Life* of Anthony, the bishop was using the hermit-saint as a mouthpiece – a way to air his personal grudges. Certainly the saint's words and actions conform very closely to his biographer's idea of the perfect Christian, but we have no way of knowing whether Athanasius distorted Anthony's life to make it fit the model he had in mind. The question of whether his biography was absolutely true in every detail may in any case have been of marginal importance to the Egyptian bishop. In his prologue written 'to the brethren in foreign parts' he stated that he wanted to write Anthony's life so that the hermit could continue to act as a model and an inspiration for future hermits and monks.

Although Athanasius may not have told the whole truth about Anthony, he probably could have done so, since, as he claims in his prologue, he had been 'his attendant for a long time, and poured water on his hands'. The close relationship between biographer and subject is something that Reginald and Godric share with Athanasius and Anthony. If it is true that Reginald failed to reveal the whole truth about Godric, it is likely that he did so for the same reasons that may have led Athanasius to 'tidy up' his account of Anthony.

In Reginald's case, this process assumes an extra dimension, in that it sometimes seems that the Durham monk, and perhaps Godric, the subject of his biography, were drawing on a long tradition of accounts of holy men that stretched back beyond Anthony and Paul of Thebes to Elijah, John the Baptist and Jesus himself. While Godric was trying to honour the tradition by living it, was his biographer trying to honour it by perpetuating it in his writings?

The tradition stated that holy hermits lived alone (or tried to live alone) in remote, inhospitable places, and responded with equanimity to privations and dangers, even turning dangerous animals into friends or servants. Despite the harsh lifestyles that they deliberately embraced, they often lived very long lives; in the cases of Godric, Paul of Thebes and Anthony of Egypt stretching beyond a century.

Though evidently very superior people with profound insights into the spiritual realm, the classic hermits were always ready to roll up their sleeves (if they had any), cultivate their own kitchen gardens, and build their own houses and chapels. These holy men and women cared nothing for clothing or other worldly goods; and when called upon to do so could give very good accounts of their faith, even if they lacked learning. They sometimes had powers of prophecy, and the link with nature that allowed them to communicate with animals also enabled them to predict changes in the weather.

They typically performed miracles, especially healing miracles, even after death, when their cherished relics were found to have miraculous powers. Paradoxically, their isolated life-styles often attracted followers. In the case of Godric and many others, their isolation did not prevent their being part of a local Christian community, which they might visit, or from which they might receive visitors.

Some were from wealthy, privileged backgrounds, and had benefited from lengthy and expensive educations. Others, like Godric, were from the classic 'poor but devout' families, and got by without much learning.

Although blessed with visions that modern readers might identify as hallucinations, hermits like Anthony never seem to have struck their contemporaries as crazy. Athanasius gives an interesting account of Anthony appearing to a crowd of people after a long period of strict isolation. On that occasion, he looked perfectly fit and well, and not even slightly under-nourished. He was not over-awed by the press of people, and spoke calmly and rationally. At the very least, this shows an adaptability in Anthony's character, something that also enabled him to abandon his hermitage from time to time to visit other places, for instance to rebuke the Arians of Alexandria, or comfort believers who were having a hard time. As the craze for monasticism spread, Anthony also found himself in the role of abbot, taking charge of a community of proto-monks.

This sense of saints as adaptable people 'for all seasons' (as was said of Saint Thomas More) is particularly marked in the case of Saint Cuthbert, who we know was a direct inspiration for Godric and was the local saint *par excellence* for much of the north of England and beyond. Cuthbert alternated between life as a hermit and life as a cenobite, or monastery monk. On one occasion the peace of his hermitage on Inner Farne was shattered by the arrival of Ecgfrith, a local king who insisted that he leave his island and become Bishop of Lindisfarne.

Although Cuthbert was born nearly three hundred years after the death of Anthony of Egypt, a native of a very different land, like Godric, who came nearly four hundred years later, he was part of the same tradition. His desert hermitage was an island in the North Sea. His hyenas were some birds who stole thatch from his roof, and had to be rebuked.

Like Elijah and Paul of Thebes, Cuthbert had experience of miraculous bread baked in heaven; and was brought food by a bird – in his case a magnificent sea-eagle gave him a fish big enough to feed the saint, his companion and the eagle herself. Like Godric, Cuthbert could predict changes in the weather, and like many holy hermits he performed miracles, many after his death. Like Anthony of Egypt, Cuthbert was blessed with a celebrated biographer: his Athanasius was the Venerable Bede, who now sleeps in Durham Cathedral's Galilee chapel, built just a few years after the death of Godric of Finchale.

Finchale at Last

Despite frequent visits to Cuthbert's shrine at Durham, it never seems to have occurred to Godric to ask one of the locals about the location of Finchale, where Cuthbert had told him he should build his hermitage. At last, by chance, he heard the place mentioned by some shepherds, when he was walking through woods near the city. The men took Godric to the place, which he found ideal for a holy retreat: it was covered in impenetrable trees and bushes, and infested with dangerous snakes.

This story, which sees Godric finding a place he had been told to find in a vision, is similar to one of the tales that surround the arrival of Cuthbert's body in Durham in the tenth century. One of the monks who were travelling with the coffin was told in a dream that the saint's remains should be taken to a place called Durham. None of Cuthbert's escorts had heard of it, but a woman who was looking for her lost cow was happy to direct them.

As he approached his future home at Finchale for the first time, Godric's way was blocked by a wolf so huge and terrifying that he knew at once that it had to be the devil in disguise. Like Anthony confronting his hyenas, Godric gave his hound from hell a good telling-off, and it soon slunk away. Later, Godric's ability to command animals, both demonic and natural, came in handy when his nephew came to live with him at Finchale. The boy was given the job of looking after Godric's cow, but he was too sleepy to be much help leading the animal to pasture at the right time, or milking her when she needed to be milked. To solve the problem, the patient uncle instructed the cow to lead *herself* to pasture and, when she felt that she needed to be milked, to come and find him, Godric, so that he could do the job.

Wild as it was, Finchale still belonged to somebody – Bishop Flambard, who as we know gave Godric permission to settle there. Godric's first hermitage was a mile or so up-river, at a place that is now called St Godric's Garth, but he soon moved to where the priory ruins are today. These stand on a piece of gently-sloping land, in a bend of the River Wear. The Wear at this point is shallow enough to walk across on most days, given a little caution and a good pair of wellington boots. There is now also a foot-bridge near the old ford.

The priory ruins are sheltered to the north and east by a high, thickly-wooded bank: this is very convenient, since the coldest winds that visit this part of the world blow from the north and east. Cleared of trees, bushes and weeds, it might have been the perfect site for a small settlement. Without all that cover, the area's notorious snakes would surely have slithered away. Why, then, had the area remained unsettled for a long time before Godric took up residence? Well, Finchale was part of land set aside for the bishop's hunting activities, and as such it was illegal to live there without permission.

Many of the old bishops of Durham were serious hunters: their hunting expeditions would go on for days on end, and could involve hundreds of people and hunting-dogs. Log-cabins were constructed to serve as temporary hunting-lodges, and there was much feasting and carousing.

Despite Godric's obligations to Flambard as his landlord, the hermit was bold and compassionate enough to frustrate one of the bishop's hunts by sheltering a magnificent stag in his little house. The whole hunt was on the tail of this great prize, but the animal knew it had a friend in Godric, and ran to him in its hour of need. By the time the hunters reached the hermit's little bend in the river, Godric's door was closed and the man himself was sitting under a tree. 'Have you seen a stag?' they asked him. 'God is the lord of all animals, wild or tame,' the hermit answered; 'surely he knows where your stag is hiding'.

At dusk, Godric helped the stag to return safely to the forest, but the friendly creature often came back, and would even spend the night lying by the hermit.

Given the violence and instability of the period, and the constant risk of Scottish raids, locals who knew about Finchale might have been reluctant to settle there, even if they had been offered the chance, because the river was too shallow to form a defensive barrier, the trees would have provided cover for raiders, and the site had no natural defences to the south and west.

These features make the site very different from Durham itself, with its peninsular nearly surrounded by the Wear, which is deeper and wider here because it is slowed down by artificial weirs. Soon after the arrival of Cuthbert's remains in 995, the whole peninsular was cleared, and for centuries no trees or bushes were allowed to grow on the banks: this made it easier for the citizens to see any approaching raiders.

Like Durham, Finchale, with its riverside setting, is vulnerable to floods. This factor might also explain why Godric's home had been innocent of human habitation for a long time before he arrived there. At Durham, floods have been known to carry off stone bridges, and when the Wear is angry, riverside paths that are usually far above the water can disappear altogether. In flood, the river becomes brown and noisy, and immense trees are washed out of its banks and carried downstream. When the water subsides, some of these are usually found leaning on the city's weirs, like drunks who have fallen asleep with their heads and elbows on the bar. Some riverside paths remain invisible because tons of silt have been dumped on them. Summer visitors often don't believe how high the water can reach.

Given that Godric lived by the Wear for over fifty years, it is hardly surprising that he lived through a number of floods. According to Reginald, he did not really witness the first of these at all. While the water was raging, he was praying all night in his chapel, oblivious to what was going on. When he emerged in the morning, he was met by some locals, led by a knight called Wilbert. They had come in search of his body, because they had seen his riverside huts completely covered by the water. This was all news to Godric – inside his chapel, everything was perfectly dry, including himself.

During another flood, Godric ordered the water not to pass a certain point on the bank. It held back, forming a wall like the walls of water that stood either side of the Israelites as they crossed the Red Sea. On another occasion, the hermit ordered the water to crash against the opposite bank. It did so, dislodging some large lumps of rock which Godric used to build a second chapel, dedicated to John the Baptist. This dedication came about because the Baptist himself appeared to Godric in a radiant vision, and suggested that the new chapel at Finchale should be dedicated to himself. Godric constructed a covered walkway – a kind of primitive cloister with a thatched roof – between the two buildings.

Peter Dunn's artist's impression of Finchale just after Godric's death in 1170, printed in Peter Ryder's book, shows the little monastic settlement with the Wear to the north and east, and a shallow ditch to the west and south. According to Dunn, this was crossed via a small wooden bridge, which could perhaps be taken up at night, or when a raid was expected. As well as slowing down any Scots, the ditch might also have kept wild animals off the monks' crops, and stopped their domestic animals wandering off into the woods. By the time of Godric's death, the site was no longer a solitary place, but housed a number of monks and others, brought there by Godric, one way or another.

The vulnerability of Finchale seems not to have bothered Godric, any more than the appearance of the demon-wolf had done. The snakes that remained after he had cleared some of the ground were not a problem for him either: he soon made friends with the reptiles, and allowed them to twist themselves round his legs, and warm themselves by his fire. The hermit's friendly attitude to these creatures is reminiscent of the Egyptian hermit Saint Agathon of Scete, a fourth-century contemporary of Saint Anthony. Moving into a desert cave, Agathon found a snake there, and naturally struck up a conversation. The snake offered to move out to make room for the holy man, but Agathon would not hear of it. He insisted that they share the cave.

There being no suitable cave at Finchale, Godric set about building a shelter. For this he used only the materials he had to hand: tree-trunks for the walls, branches for the roof-beams and turf for the roof itself. The roof would probably have had a large hole in the centre to let out smoke from Godric's fire. The newcomer also fashioned a door, presumably from planks cut from raw forest wood. He would have needed an axe or axes for this work, and perhaps an adze or a saw. He would also have needed a spade to cut the turf for his roof. Like most of the poor peasants in Norman times, Godric would have had a bare earth floor.

Most modern people would struggle to build such a hut, but his background as a Norfolk farm-boy would have equipped Godric with a range of useful skills, some of which may have been completely lost to our high-tech age. The hermit also had the advantage of being physically very strong. Reginald tells us that when he was clearing the ground at Finchale, he pulled up the roots of an oak-tree, a task that four men of average strength would have found daunting.

In his first home at Finchale, Godric might sometimes have been more comfortable than the Norman rulers of the time, some of whom lived in draughty stone castles. Like the larger peasants' cottages of the Norman period, with their thatched roofs and wattle-and-daub walls, Godric's hut would have needed constant attention and regular maintenance.

Later the hermit built a larger structure, which was part home and part chapel. Hidden under the floor of the new house was a deep earthenware pot full of cold water, in which Godric would immerse himself, to mortify his flesh. The 'house' side of the building featured a flat stone, which Godric used as a table during the day, and a pillow at night.

It may seem odd that Godric may have felt that he needed cold water in his house, when he had the River Wear right on his doorstep (not that he would have had a doorstep). It may be that at times the river was too shallow for full immersion, or was frozen solid right to the bottom. When the Wear was merely frozen over, Godric would break the ice and immerse himself up to the neck as usual.

The hermit might also have been shy about bathing in this way when there might have been other people around who could see him. This may have been modesty, but it may also have sprung from a desire not to risk building up his pride – a dangerous thing for a trainee saint – by making the details of his holy habits known. At times Godric may have needed his chilly ceramic bath because the river was flowing too swiftly, and threatened to sweep him away.

As often with Godric, his practices can be traced back to his beloved Saint Cuthbert. Cuthbert is known to have prayed for hours on end while immersed not in a river but in the North Sea. In one story, an unseen witness follows him to the beach and sees him emerge from the water after a whole night of praying among the waves. A pair of sea-otters intercepted the saint and proceeded to dry his feet with their fur.

Why did Godric feel that he needed to make himself suffer through all these self-imposed hardships? It seems that, though his soul was yearning for a purer way of life, and ultimately for admittance to heaven, his body, and perhaps his heart and mind, sometimes pulled him in a different direction. On bad days he yearned for company, especially female company, and for better food and living conditions. In medieval times it was thought that these yearnings, which could distract seekers after holiness from the right path, could be suppressed by giving the body a hard time. Godric not only immersed himself in cold water; he starved himself, went without sleep and even threw himself into thorn bushes, emerging covered with scratches and scars. He also wrecked his skin by continuing to wear a hair shirt, which he allowed to become infested with fleas and lice.

At first Godric wore a heavy chain on top of his hair shirt, to add to his discomfort. This later became a proper coat of chain-mail, of the type worn by knights at the time, fashioned from hundreds of iron links. This must have weighed about seven kilograms, or fifteen pounds, the weight of a bowling-ball, or a five-month-old baby. At some point, as his contacts with the Benedictine monks of Durham became more frequent, the hermit began to wear a monk's habit, presumably under his chain-mail.

Although it is widely known that Godric wore chain-mail for many years, he is not usually depicted wearing it. I have only been able to find one picture of him wearing any kind of armour: a humble prayer-card where he is shown with his tame snakes, wearing a sort of chain-mail collar.

According to Reginald, the devil knew how sorely the hermit was tempted, and sent him visions of beautiful women to distract him. One of these sat down next to him and started to accuse him of being a woman-hater. He assured 'her' that he loved and respected women, but had no time at all for demons disguised as women. One story of Godric's good relations with women also demonstrates his ability to see into the future, and even involves Ranulf Flambard's bridge across the Wear at Durham, which at that time would have been very new.

A noblewoman came to see Godric, oppressed by many problems. The hermit was considerate enough to see her alone, with nobody else in ear-shot. It transpired that all of her troubles were centred around the long absence of her husband, whom she feared might be dead. Without him, she found it hard to manage their estates, and she was coming off worst in legal disputes about their property. Godric reassured her, saying that she would soon meet a brave soldier on a bridge, and that he would solve all her problems. The soldier was of course her husband, returned from his travels, and the bridge was Flambard's Framwellgate Bridge.

Like the wolf that was too big to be a real wolf, Godric was sometimes able to recognise the demon behind the disguise thanks to some physical characteristic. At other times, he could spot demons because of what they said, or didn't say. A demon that came in the shape of a pious pilgrim gave itself away by boasting too much about the hardships it had supposedly suffered on its pilgrimages. Another demon, that begged the hermit for some of his apples, betrayed itself because it could not say the word 'love'. Godric dealt with these demons either by ignoring them, calmly praying while they were present, or by pronouncing holy words such as the name of Jesus, which they could not bear to hear. The hermit also scared them off by showing them crosses, or illustrations from his holy books. Then the demons would reveal their true selves by reverting to their proper, hideous shapes, or by giving off an offensive stench.

At times, the same demons that gave Godric a hard time would also harm his friend Roger, the prior of Durham. The demons were quite able to beat Godric up, and trash his chapel, leaving his holy equipment scattered on the floor.

Godric could spot when other people were being troubled by demons, and could even see evil spirits that were invisible to everyone else. When a fight broke out between two men who were attending a service in his chapel, their host could spot the mischievous imp that was spurring them on. And when somebody turned up late for a meeting at Finchale, Godric knew he was telling the truth when he said his horse had been acting up. The hermit could not only see the fractious horse using his remote vision – he could also see that it was being distracted by a demon.

His war against the demons, and against what we might call his natural self, was the great conflict of Godric's life. In this context, Reginald calls him a 'soldier' and depicts the banks of the Wear at Finchale as the theatre of an epic clash between good and evil. The fact that he wore chain-mail, part of a knight's outfit, brings the military analogy into sharper focus.

When Godric was not actually fasting, his diet at Finchale was by no means ample or appetising. At first he is supposed to have lived on river-water, and edible herbs from the forest. In spring these would have included wild garlic, which grows in profusion along the banks of the Wear even today. The hermit could also have feasted on chickweed, dandelions, nettles, horse parsley and sweet violet. If he included fruit, nuts and fungi in his diet, Godric might have lived quite well, especially at certain times of the year. He would, however, have needed to be able to tell edible plants and fungi from poisonous ones, when best to pick his plants, and how to render toxic foodstuffs like acorns safe for human consumption.

The woods that he was using as his larder would also have been less useful if other people were regularly picking through them for 'bush tucker'. Since the land had been given to him by its owner, the bishop of Durham, any such people might have been breaking the law by straying onto Godric's domain. In those days, pigs were often reared in forests, but a fairly small number of these, if introduced, would surely have emptied Godric's natural larder in just a few days.

As Francis Rice pointed out, Godric was turning his back on an excellent source of nutrition by refusing to fish in his bit of river, and refraining from hunting or trapping animals such as rabbits, wild boar, beavers and deer. These animals might also have provided the saint with skins to wear. In later years, when Godric had to entertain many visitors at Finchale, he set up fish-traps merely to provide nourishment for his guests. Both visitors and servants were repeatedly astonished at how many large, good-quality fish would be found in these traps, even in summer when the river had shrunk to a tiny stream.

Godric might also have kept bees at Finchale, which would have made him like the speaker of W.B. Yeats's poem *The Lake Isle of Innisfree* (1888):

> I will arise and go now, and go to Innisfree,
> And a small cabin build there, of clay and wattles made;
> Nine bean-rows will I have there, a hive for the honey-bee,
> And live alone in the bee-loud glade.

Yeats's poem captures a modern version of the would-be hermit's yearning for a humble waterside retreat; a yearning that is also encapsulated in Henry David Thoreau's book *Walden* (1854).

Thoreau lived for two years in a self-built cabin in the woods by Walden Pond, near Concord, Massachusetts.

Although Godric was in effect hiding at Finchale, news of his arrival soon spread among the local people, and they began to bring him gifts of food. These he either ignored altogether, gave to the poor or offered as sacrifices to God. The woodland animals would surely have eaten the food the hermit offered as part of a prayerful service, though Godric believed that it was sometimes taken up into heaven by angels.

The locals who had been kind enough to donate food to Godric changed their attitude when he accidentally tried to grow crops on what they regarded as common land, set aside as a place for them to graze their domestic animals. They waited until his corn was ready to harvest, then deliberately sent in their animals to eat it. Their owners soon learned that it does not pay to attack a holy man. Godric's wrecked crop grew back in double-quick time, and like Jesus' miraculous draught of fishes, exceeded all expectations.

Godric's grain crop and fruit trees were also attacked by wild animals, including deer and rabbits. These he rebuked, in true saintly style, and then proceeded to help them find their way out of his compound. He reminded the rabbits that God had provided food for them in the forest, and they never returned.

The hermit-smallholder was not so stern when poor people asked him for food, or when they begged for something he owned to take away as a pious memento. Since he had so few possessions, he often gave them some bread of his own making, or apples from his orchard. These items were found to have miraculous properties: for instance they could heal people who were on the brink of dying of terrible diseases. Other gifts from Godric, such as an old belt or even a tuft of his beard, could help with medical problems such as fevers, dysentery, infertility in women or the tendency of a woman to miscarry.

Home-grown organic grain and fruit, and the best of the food foraged from the surrounding landscape, may sound appetising, but, as he had done on his last pilgrimage to the Holy Land, Godric was determined to make his food as unpalatable as possible. He waited until his bread was stale and his fruit rotten before he ate them, and mixed dirt and ashes into his recipes. As a result, his stomach protested, but he rebuked it as he had the creatures that had raided his crops.

While Godric had plenty to say *to* his stomach, Nicholas Breakspear, one of the hermit's more interesting contemporaries, used the stomach as a metaphor in a dialogue with his friend, the philosopher John of Salisbury. Breakspear, a Hertfordshire man, was the only English Roman Catholic pope there has ever been, unless you believe that an English woman became Pope Joan at some point in the ninth century. During his short pontificate, which lasted from 1154 to 1159, John of Salisbury visited Breakspear, who had taken the name Adrian IV upon his election. John asked Nicholas how the papacy could justify its immense wealth. Adrian replied that the papacy was like the stomach of a human being, which seems to get all the food, but naturally distributes its goodness to the rest of the body. This image was used by William Shakespeare in the first scene of his play *Coriolanus*.

War and Miracles

For some of the years when Godric was fighting his spiritual battles by the River Wear at Finchale, a disastrous civil war was raging all around him. The roots of the conflict lay in a terrible accident that happened in the winter of 1120, when Godric would have been in his fifties.

The tragedy was the accidental sinking of the *White Ship* off Barfleur in Normandy. Among the three hundred or so passengers who perished were William Adelin, the only legitimate son of the English King Henry I. Several of Henry's illegitimate children were also drowned. Orderic Vitalis, one of the few contemporary chroniclers who did not have 'of' as his middle name, blamed the shipwreck on the drunkenness of the sailors. Henry of Huntingdon suggested that many of the victims deserved to drown because they were sodomites. Orderic tells us that Stephen of Blois, the future King Stephen of England, disembarked before the *White Ship* set off, because he was too drunk to travel.

The loss of his son William meant that Henry had to make a decision about the succession. His only surviving legitimate heir was a girl, Matilda, who had been married off to the German emperor at the age of twelve, in 1114. Her imperial husband died in 1125, and in 1126 Matilda's father made the great and the good of his kingdom swear to uphold her claim to the English throne. In 1128, Matilda married Count Geoffrey of Anjou. Having been married herself for the first time at the age of twelve, she now married a boy of fifteen: by this time, she would have been in her mid-twenties.

When Matilda's father King Henry I of England died in Normandy in 1135, many of those who had sworn to uphold Matilda's succession forgot their vow and transferred their allegiance to the aforementioned Stephen of Blois, who returned to England from France very soon after the death of his royal uncle Henry I.

The Anglo-Saxon Chronicle is very clear about the state of England under Stephen. All over the country, wealthy magnates built castles, which they filled with 'devils and evil men'. These warlords, taking advantage of the general collapse of authority, imprisoned and tortured anyone they imagined had wealth, and lawlessness was so prevalent that it was hard to tell officials like sheriffs and reeves from common brigands.

The first few years of King Stephen's reign were relatively peaceful, at least for England, but soon after Matilda and her half-brother Robert of Gloucester invaded in 1138, the king and his enemies found themselves endlessly travelling around the country, followed by armies of various sizes, besieging castles, towns and cities, or being besieged; building new castles, demolishing castles, towns and cities, being taken prisoner, being released from captivity, and, sometimes, negotiating truces, exchanges, alliances and other deals.

At times, Stephen must have felt like a man parts of whose house keep bursting into flames. He is forever hurrying around with his fire-extinguisher, but as soon as one fire is out, a new one starts up. Meanwhile he is getting older and more weary, and, despite his attempts to re-build, the general state of the house is getting worse and worse. To extend the analogy of England as an inflammable house, Stephen's situation was made worse by the fact that his enemies, and even some neutral onlookers, believed that he should not be in possession of his house at all.

To make matters even worse, members of his own family were among those who were straining every sinew to try to evict him. Matilda was the daughter of his mother's brother, and her powerful ally and half-brother Robert of Gloucester was, like Matilda and Stephen, descended from King William I. On one level the civil war that raged through much of Stephen's reign was, therefore, a deadly version of one of those prolonged family rows about property and inheritance.

According to Henry of Huntingdon, the stress of the war caused the familiar Christian calendar to be neglected, so that it no longer seemed to matter whether it was Christmas or Easter. Peace had vanished, as had the vast wealth Stephen had inherited from his predecessor Henry I. Arson, murder, pillage and destruction were the order of the day. Everywhere the sounds of terror and lamentation were heard, and everywhere people were starving. Crime was rampant, and not even women or priests were spared. Robbers looted churches and held priests for ransom. Who was to bury the piles of dead? The state of the country reminded the chronicler of the fabled Styx, a river in Hell.

Where some see chaos and mayhem, others spot opportunities. As we know, King David I of Scotland invaded England in the summer of 1138, ostensibly to lend the weight of his arms to the cause of his niece, the empress Matilda. He also thought that his incursion might gain him some more territory to rule over and, like Baldwin I of Jerusalem, he no doubt judged that success in battle might win him a better reputation, and further legitimate his claim to the Scottish throne. Like most European armies of this time, and all armies for many centuries to come, the chance of booty would also have been a major motivation for David's troops.

Hearing the news of this new Scottish invasion, King Stephen, still rushing around with his metaphorical fire-extinguisher, was no doubt completely exasperated. Everybody knew that King David of Scotland owed a lot to Anglo-Normans like Stephen. As a young man in exile from his own country, he had found shelter at the court of the English King Henry I. David had fought for and won the Scottish crown with the backing of King Henry. As king, he had tried to re-model Scotland along Anglo-Norman lines. Tied up with conflicts further south, Stephen was only able to send a small force of his own to meet the Scots, and did not travel north in person.

The economy and life in general in England's northern counties had suffered for many years because of the incursions of the Scots. These ranged from small raids by cattle-rustlers to full-blown invasions, including those led by King David, not only in 1138 but also in 1135 and 1137. Even after his defeat at the Battle of the Standard, of which more later, David continued to take advantage of the chaotic political situation south of the border for many years.

In 1138, David quickly overran much of Northumberland, capturing castles, towns, cities and monasteries. Many settlements meekly yielded up their treasures and food-supplies rather than be besieged and perhaps demolished. Despite this, there were many atrocities: women and children were stripped, tied together and hauled off to a life of slavery. Men, women and children were murdered, and according to Henry of Huntingdon, some of the Scots killed pregnant women by ripping their babies out of their bellies. It was said that small children were also thrown into the air and caught on the ends of spears.

As if in a parody of atrocities allegedly committed by the Muslim invaders of the Holy Land, priests were dismembered by the Scots on their own altars. Henry tells us that the heads were cut off crucifixes and replaced with the heads of murdered priests.

Severed heads were also placed on holy altars, thus defiling them, and the invaders dared to trample the communion bread underfoot, as they had in Godric's oratory. In a shocking parody of the Mass, the raiders drank water mixed with human blood, and turned churches and chapels into stables and brothels. For some chroniclers, the re-purposing of churches and cathedrals into castles was one of the more disturbing practices of the combatants in England's twelfth-century civil war.

If it was some disorderly offshoot of David's army that visited Godric at Finchale in 1138, then it would seem that the hermit got off lightly. As we have seen, Aelred of Rievaulx wrote an account of this particular Scottish invasion, but his resulting text shows signs of an attempt to be diplomatic. Aelred was, after all, a friend and admirer of the Scottish king, and as a young man had spent several years at the Scottish court.

How, then, to account for the atrocities of the Scots? Aelred decided to blame these on one section of the Scottish host, the notoriously wild Galwegians, or men of Galloway in the southwest. In his account, Aelred attributes many of the atrocities to them alone: they are scarcely human, beasts, loathed and cursed by heaven, earth and the sea. They have only survived so that the English can enjoy the glory of killing them. Evidently, the good work Saint Ninian had done among these people in the fifth century had not had a lasting effect on every member of the population.

The abbot of Rievaulx makes it clear that the Scottish king was full of remorse over what the Galwegians had done. He trembled, wept, struck his breast and cried out to hear of their atrocities, which went clean against his own orders to his troops. It seems that he was having the same problems controlling his diverse host as Peter the Hermit had had keeping those First Crusaders under his thumb. Elements of David's army, such as his highly-trained, well-equipped elite knights, were tightly disciplined, but other elements resembled a riot or a rabble on the move, or a plague of locusts.

Concerned about his chances of success against the English, and in fear of his own life, David probably did not have the time, the intelligence network, the communications system or the command structure to ensure that foraging did not become pillaging, and what we would now call martial law did not become violent oppression.

Aelred's account is called *The Battle of the Standard*, after the engagement that was the climax of this particular Scottish invasion. The battle was so called because the English set up a standard on a cart: from the standard hung holy banners from Durham, York, Beverly and Ripon, and a box containing the consecrated wafers used in the Eucharist. The gesture is reminiscent of the saintly King Oswald of Northumbria, who set up an improvised cross at the Battle of Heavenfield in 633 or 634. Oswald's head is said to rest in Cuthbert's coffin under the flagstones of Durham Cathedral.

On the eve of the Battle of the Standard, which took place near Northallerton in August 1138, the unruly Galwegians caused even more problems for the Scottish king. It seems that they were filled with a sort of macho recklessness or bloodthirsty over-confidence. They insisted on being placed at the front of David's troops for the first attack, though they had no armour and only flimsy spears. They were up against English knights fighting on foot, and ranks of English archers. The results were entirely predictable. After such a poor start, the Scottish army slowly crumbled, and David was forced to retreat.

The defeat near Northampton did not prevent the Scottish king from continuing to interfere in English affairs. One of his interventions involved Godric's home turf of Durham, the city's priory and cathedral. When Bishop Geoffrey Rufus of Durham died in 1141, his clerk, William Cumin, forced himself into the position of bishop, with the backing of his old friend King David I. His appointment had no basis in church law and had not been approved by the pope or either of the English archbishops. According to the continuation of Simeon of Durham's history of the church of Durham, Cumin 'the intruder' spent his time as phoney bishop extracting as much wealth from the diocese as he possibly could. His dastardly soldiers were given free reign to torture the better-off locals until they agreed to surrender their treasures. Joseph Stevenson's translation tells us that the appearance of the city of Durham under Cumin:

. . . was wretched, for every house within its walls exhibited traces of tortures having been inflicted, just as if the tyrants of all bygone ages had congregated therein. In one place you might see some extended upon the rack, some were suspended by their privy members, some were shut up within little chests with stones beneath them, and nearly crushed to death.

Attempts by the rightful bishop, William of St Barbara, to take possession of his see led to open warfare between the two sides: one of the casualties was Ranulf Flambard's Kepier Hospital, which was burned to the ground.

The civil war dragged on until 1153. It was in that year that David I of Scotland died, on the twenty-fourth of May. In the year after that, King Stephen exited from this world at Dover in Kent. Although Stephen's rival the empress Matilda never reigned as queen, her son assumed the throne after Stephen's death. This had been agreed by treaty in 1153, a deal that ended the civil war but disinherited Stephen's oldest surviving son, William. The new king was Henry II.

The Scots who threatened Godric were not the only group of desperate marauders that was thrown up by the chaotic circumstances of the twelfth-century civil war in England. An English band led by a local man called Elferus was made up of men who had been pillaged into total poverty, and were desperate enough to try anything just to survive. Believing, like the Scots, that Godric had some kind of treasure concealed in his home, they set off for Finchale. Night fell, and soon it seemed to them that they had been tramping through the forest for hours. When dawn came, they found that they had been going round in circles all night.

Even Godric succumbed to the idea that there might be treasure (which even he didn't know about) buried at Finchale. He was persuaded of this by a dream, but when he started digging, thinking to give any treasure he found to the poor, hundreds of scary little demons appeared, and started throwing stink-bombs at him. Although he remained convinced that they were guarding treasure, Godric filled in his hole and never tried to dig for treasure again.

Sometimes Godric's visitors demanded rather more than gold and jewels. Once, a distraught young couple appeared with a mysterious sack. This was during Godric's early days as a hermit at Finchale, when he could be very gruff and unsociable. He ignored them and went about his own business. Eventually they forced their own business on the holy man. The sack contained their dead daughter: would Godric bury her, or better still, bring her back to life? Still the hermit gave them the silent treatment, and at last they went away, but left the little girl in her sack in Godric's chapel.

Unsure how to proceed, Godric turned to prayer. After three gruelling days on his knees, the hermit heard the little girl wandering around near his chapel. He summoned the parents and swore them to secrecy: they should not mention the miracle to anyone until he, Godric, was dead. As a result this, one of the greatest miracles Godric performed during his life, only came to light when the hermit was telling his story to the monk, Reginald.

But it is hard to imagine how the parents of the little girl could have kept quiet about the miracle. Wouldn't friends, relatives or neighbours of the parents have known that their little girl had died? What did they think when her parents brought the girl home, alive and well? The girl-in-the-sack miracle was confirmed after Godric's death when the grateful parents, now released from their oath, began to tell their own version of the story.

After Godric's death another couple emerged, this time from Northumberland, telling a similar tale about their son, whom Godric had also raised from the dead, although at the time he had insisted that the child was not dead at all. Their narrative had an extra dimension, because the mother of the little boy had been childless until she had begged Godric to cure her infertility. This he did, on condition that the child be called Godric, and considered to be his own son.

No doubt the satirical Robert Hegge, or the scurrilous John Aubrey, would have suggested that Godric had helped the woman get pregnant in the traditional way. Women have often found that though they cannot conceive a child with one man, such as their husband, they can get pregnant after sleeping with someone else.

Even without this suggestion, the story of the origins of Godric's 'son' is arresting. Did the hermit's desire to adopt the child of the couple from Northumberland, even before its conception, arise out of a sense of regret at never having fathered any children of his own? Whatever his motivation, the story is like a Christian version of some dark folk-tale where a childless couple are given a child on the understanding that it will never be truly theirs, and may be snatched away from them at any time via supernatural means. Superman, the comic-book hero who first appeared in 1938, is an interstellar orphan with magical powers who falls into the hands of a childless couple, the Kents of the imaginary American town of Smallville.

Aspects of the stories of the resurrections of dead children by the power of Godric's prayers will be familiar to readers of the New Testament. Matthew, Mark and Luke tell us that Jesus restored the twelve year-old daughter of Jairus to life, though in the Gospels it is implied that the girl has only just died. In any case Jesus tells everyone present that she is not dead, but only sleeping. As if to prove that he could resurrect someone who had been dead for rather longer, Jesus called Lazarus from his tomb after four days. Like the girl Godric's prayers restored to life, Jesus himself was dead for three days between his crucifixion and resurrection.

It would seem that it was some years after Godric's resurrection miracle that he managed to perform almost the opposite miracle. This time, the loving parents were not given the cold shoulder when they came to see Godric, but were welcomed by the hermit, who spent the evening chatting to them. When they made to go, Godric insisted that they stay a little longer: this he did several times. When the couple finally set off for their home at Haswell, they learned that their son had died while they were absent. The hermit had seen this happening, via his saintly power of remote vision, and wanted to save his guests the pain of seeing their child die.

Godric's prayers and his closeness to God could also assist people after death. Both his mother and his brother William moved to live closer to him in their later years, and the hermit prayed for them fervently after their deaths. He was rewarded with visions of them in heaven: his prayers had rescued them from purgatory. By contrast, his pious sister Burcwen had gone straight to heaven. This is hardly surprising, since for some years she had lived near him at Finchale, as a sort of female counterpart to her pious brother. After death, she visited Godric in the form of a radiant vision.

Monks, Music and More Miracles

It seems that Godric was able to live independently at Finchale for a while, although, as we have seen, local animals and people would visit him from time to time. His presence there would not, however, have been sustainable without the initial permission to use the land that he had been granted by Bishop Flambard, and as time went on, the involvement of the monks of Durham Priory in his life became more and more important.

The Durham brothers, who used the cathedral as their priory church, were Benedictines, but they had not always been. William de St-Calais, who became bishop after Bishop Walcher was murdered at Gateshead, felt that what might, to the untrained eye, have seemed like a monastic community at Durham was in fact nothing of the sort.

The Anglo-Saxon *Congregatio* consisted of a dean and a number of priests and clerks who seem not to have lived according to any monastic rule, and even had wives and families. They were the successors of the people who had rescued Cuthbert's body from Lindisfarne, and had watched over the sacred remains for many years until they reached their final home at Durham. Bishop William was determined to remove these individuals, though he did not leave them homeless and destitute. Only one of them agreed to cross over and embrace a new life of strict discipline and celibacy.

The new bishop was not forced to import 'proper' monks into Durham from any remote region. A Benedictine community had already established itself, literally in the ruins of the deserted monasteries of Jarrow and Wearmouth, which Bede had known and written about. These men were moved out of the rough huts they had built against the rugged walls of the old monasteries, and placed in new accommodation at Durham.

By the time Godric started his new life at Finchale, the priory at Durham had been a Benedictine house for over thirty years. It may have been over twenty years after that that the hermit became formally attached to the monastery, since we know that these closer relations were associated with Godric's good friend Prior Roger, who probably became prior around 1138.

Godric was by no means the only hermit attached in some way to the monks of Durham. There were others on the Farne islands, living something like the life Saint Cuthbert had lived in the same place in the seventh century. Francis Rice characterises Godric's embrace by the Durham prior and his monks as a wholly good thing – a win-win for everybody involved. The holy brothers taught Godric to divide his days and weeks according to something like their Benedictine rule; observing periods of silence during which he was obliged to communicate via sign language, if at all. Priests from Durham would arrive to celebrate services with the hermit, and it seems that the monks were able to persuade Godric to cut down on some of the excessive hard-living to which he had been subjecting himself.

Together with the more regulated Godric, who gladly accepted friendship and advice from others, a new, more affable hermit was emerging. Whereas stories such as that of the miracle of the little girl in the sack exhibit the gruff, taciturn Godric, accounts that seem to come from later in his life show him enjoying whole days in company, and not just with monks. Access to him was, however, controlled by the Durham brothers, who may thus have helped him to avoid being overwhelmed with casual and curious visitors, as his reputation grew. People who wished to see Godric now had to sue for permission at Durham. If they were successful, they were given a distinctive small wooden cross, which acted as a kind of ticket, passport or certificate. In theory, the hermit would only speak to people who had this token, so that in effect his visitors were 'vetted'.

The restrictions on visitors did not mean that Godric might now find himself alone at Finchale, from time to time. On the contrary, not only monks, including his biographer Reginald, but also a small staff of servants seem to have taken up either permanent, temporary or occasional residence at or near Finchale, including small boys who were expected to work for their living, in those days before compulsory education. It may be that Godric was not the ideal master for a gang of servants, however small. The fact that he was often rewarded by heavenly visions, and also assailed by demons, meant that all sorts of strange sounds would issue from his little house, and his supernatural gift of seeing things at a distance meant that any attempt to cheat him, steal from him or cut corners could end in extreme embarrassment for the perpetrators. He also tended to win every argument, thanks to his far-seeing, his gift of prophecy and his innate wisdom.

As Godric grew older, both monks and lay-servants joined forces to nurse him through at least eight years of chronic illness. During this time, he seldom stirred from his bed, and though Reginald may have been exaggerating the pain and incapacity he experienced, if he had to endure a quarter of what his biographer described, then the elderly hermit must have presented a pitiful spectacle.

The man who had long tormented his body with celibacy, bad food, freezing water, thorn-bushes and a stone pillow now found that his body was tormenting him. For years, he was afflicted with painful swellings throughout his frame. Modern medics call this oedema: it used to be called dropsy. Reginald himself may have suffered from something like this, which Godric quickly cured with the touch of his hands. One wonders if there was some factor at Finchale itself that caused the two men to suffer a similar health problem.

A 2021 article by Stephen Martin in the journal *Hektoen International* suggests that Godric may have caught small pox, and that the sores or 'pustules' that would have appeared on his skin then became infected with a bacterium picked up from a dirty puddle or similar source. The same thing could have happened to Reginald. Whatever ailed Godric, his case was not as tractable as Reginald's had been: his biographer describes how Godric's swellings had to be regularly drained or 'milked', a painful procedure which brought only temporary relief.

Oedema is not a disease in itself but can be a symptom of a number of health issues, including heart problems and a range of different infections. Old people are particularly prone to it – Godric may have been in his late nineties when oedema laid him low. The fact that his swellings could be 'milked' suggests that Godric's oedema had given rise to ulcers – a sign that the problem had got out of control. If Godric had swelling but no ulcers then the 'milking' Reginald refers to might have been old-fashioned medicinal blood-letting.

For older patients, oedema can present them with a classic vicious circle: movement is painful because of the swellings, yet a sedentary lifestyle is bad for the circulation; and bad circulation can be a contributory factor to oedema. If Godric survived with an ulcerating form of oedema for several years, that is either a tribute to his physical toughness, or to the care supplied by his attendants, or both.

Today a physician would probe Godric for the underlying cause of his oedema and proceed accordingly. One suspects that the culprit in Godric's case was some kind of infection: in the twenty-first century, a course antibiotics might be indicated. In the eleventh century, Avicenna had correctly identified kidney problems as one cause of dropsy, and in his *Canon of Medicine* he listed a range of substances that could be used to treat it. Modern medicine has discovered that many of these have anti-inflammatory properties. The Persian polymath's list includes the maidenhair fern, cannabis, castor oil, chamomile, tamarisk, hazel, saffron, caraway, lettuce and the humble apple. Some of these substances would have been easy for a twelfth-century doctor based in Durham to get hold of, but we just don't know if any of them, or anything other than the 'milking' procedure, were tried on Godric.

In his last illness, Godric continued to be plagued by demons, including the devil himself. Whole swarms of satanic creatures appeared to him in many ludicrous shapes, hoping to benefit from his weak condition. They crowded his little buildings, mocking him, threatening him with an eternal afterlife in hell, and even dragging him out of bed and throwing him on the floor. But the hermit was also vastly comforted by visits from various heavenly beings, including the Virgin Mary and John the Baptist.

There is no doubt that his visions of saints, and of his dead sister, were seen by Godric as immense benefits conferred on him by the grace of God. Among other positives to come out of these encounters were the English-language songs that the Virgin Mary, Mary Magdalen, Burcwen and others were good enough to teach him during their visits. The words of three of these songs were written down, probably by Reginald, together with a form of musical notation. This may make them the earliest English songs for which we have both words and music, which is partly why they have gained Godric a generous entry in Grove (The New Grove Dictionary of Music and Musicians). The titles of Godric's songs are *Sainte Marie virgine moder alone*, *Kyrieleyson: Crist and Sainte Marie* and *Sainte Nicholaes, Godes druð* (meaning God's beloved). A fourth song, *Welcume Symond*, was never properly recorded, and is now lost.

Reginald tells us that Godric was 'entirely ignorant of music', but it seems that he could keep an original song in his head long enough to sing it to Reginald, or someone else who could then attempt to capture it on parchment. One of the songs was taught to him by the Virgin Mary herself, at the end of a lengthy episode during which both the Virgin and Mary Magdalen appeared to Godric as glowing, radiant creatures.

The language of the songs' lyrics is the English of the twelfth century. It has a decidedly Germanic look and sound – this was Old English the language of the Anglo-Saxons, which would change over time as the Normans introduced more French words. Here is the opening verse from Godric's hymn to Saint Nicholas, the saint who would eventually evolve into Father Christmas:

Sainte Nicholaes godes druð
tymbre us faire scone hus
At þi burth at þi bare
Sainte nicholaes bring vs wel þare

The lines printed above include two letters that are now lost to English: 'ð' or eth, which makes a 'dh' sound, and 'þ', the thorn, for 'th'. At the beginning of the second line Godric uses the word 'tymbre' as a verb, meaning 'to build'. 'Scone hus' on the same line means 'good house', 'scone' being similar to the modern German 'schön', meaning beautiful. The lyricist is therefore asking

Saint Nicholas to 'build us a fair, beautiful house'. He then goes on to beg the saint to bring us safely to this house 'at þi burth at þi bare', meaning 'at our birth, and when we are lying on the bier'. The strangeness of the English makes it difficult to pick out many words when Godric's songs are sung in the original language.

A version of all three, recorded by the early music ensemble Sequentia, is freely available online. Sequentia's interpretation sounds as if it was recorded in a Norman cathedral, or similar space, and it immediately evokes that world of high, round-topped arches, flickering candles, and monks chanting into the gloom. What Reginald wrote down were monophonies – he was recording a single, unaccompanied voice. Although Sequentia's version is also unaccompanied, their arrangement includes both male and female voices, and occasional harmonies.

Beautiful, sombre and strange as it is, this is not the sound of a lone hermit singing his heart out by a river in the open air. Sequentia's recording is a reminder that, though he was at first unique, eccentric and independent, Godric's life (and in this case his songs) became associated with monks, monasticism and Latin Christianity in general. His message was written down and brought inside, into the cloister; it was domesticated – but was something lost in the process? And were things added that had nothing to do with Godric at all?

The idea that Godric's songs were inspired by beings from heaven is reminiscent of the story of Caedmon, a contemporary of Saint Cuthbert, who was a lay brother at Whitby Abbey in Yorkshire. Like Godric, Caedmon was also quite ignorant of music, but became an inspired song-writer after experiencing a dream where a mysterious individual told him to sing a song about no less a subject than creation itself.

In recent years, partly because of increased interest in women's contributions to the arts, Hildegard of Bingen has become the best-known European musical composer of the twelfth century. This German abbess, who was born around 1098, was far more prolific as a composer than her older contemporary Godric, and also distinguished herself as a writer. Like Godric, her first Latin primer had been a psalter. Also like Godric, she saw visions, and was interested in medicine, about which she wrote two works; *Physica* and *Causae et Curae*. Among other cures, Hildegard recommended live glow-worms (trapped in a bag and applied to the stomach) for epilepsy; and a sapphire, sucked briefly every morning, to heighten intelligence.

Another connection between the German abbess and the hermit of Finchale is formed by the links in a chain of friendships. Hildegard knew Bernard of Clairvaux and, as we know, Godric knew Aelred of Rievaulx, who in turn was a friend and colleague of Bernard. Bernard was among those with whom Hildegard kept up a copious correspondence. She also exchanged letters with the German emperor Frederick Barbarossa, and the English pope, Adrian IV. Many of the great and good turned to Hildegard for advice, as they also turned to Godric. Like Godric, Hildegard also performed miracles.

Hildegard had lived with Jutta, a German anchoress, but it is unlikely that she would have lasted long as a hermit at a place like Finchale. She did not enjoy anything like Godric's rude health, being sickly much of the time. As the daughter of an aristocratic house, she might also have lacked the skills Godric used to make a life for himself in a wild setting.

It was in his chapel dedicated to the Baptist that Godric finally died, at the incredible age of one hundred and five, on the twenty-first of May 1170. The Durham Benedictines immediately began to prepare his body for a burial in the style of a monk of their order. On the day of the funeral, huge crowds appeared, and the body of the frail old man was laid to rest under the floor of the chapel where he had died. The site is now marked with a modest stone cross set in the grass that now surrounds the ruins of the priory that was later built on the site.

Relics of Godric, including links from his chain-mail shirt, were found to have healing properties: even water in which they had been immersed performed miraculous cures when drunk by ailing believers. We have already seen how, even during his life, items associated with the hermit could perform miracles. Sick people, and those with various disabilities and impairments, also got better after visiting Godric's hermitage at Finchale, which continued to be home to a small community of monks and lay-brothers after Godric's death.

The place became particularly noted for restoring sight to the blind. In one case a blind woman found that she could see perfectly when she was half-way across the Wear, wading over to get to Godric's old stamping-ground. She opted, very wisely, not to turn back, but to continue to the hermitage to give thanks to the late saint, and to visit his grave. Sometimes pilgrims whose sight was restored by Godric's posthumous influence saw a vision of the hermit himself when they first opened their eyes.

Although the woman whose sight was restored mid-river was probably crossing via the ford, another woman crossed at a deep and dangerous spot. This was a symptom of the mental illness from which she was suffering, and she soon became one of the many people with psychiatric problems who were cured after a visit to Godric's riverside shrine. The site proved popular as a place of pilgrimage for women in general, perhaps because they were not permitted to approach Cuthbert's tomb in Durham Cathedral.

The shrine also became known as a place where oedema, from which Godric himself had suffered, could be cured. A number of lepers also cast off their condition after a visit. These instant cures of leprosy are particularly surprising, as the disease usually takes a long time to get better, even under treatment with modern medicines. In one case, Godric, like a modern GP working as part of a healthcare network, referred a young girl with leprosy to a nearby hospital. This cannot have been Sherburn Hospital near Durham, which was only founded as a leper-house in 1181, eleven years after the hermit's death. It may have been an earlier institution of the same type, at Baydale near Darlington. According to the aforementioned article by Stephen Martin, published in *Hektoen International* in 2021, part of this building may still be in use, as a public house.

Although there were patients with leprosy in England much earlier, there was an alarming rise in cases in England and throughout Western Europe in the twelfth century. This has been attributed to Crusaders bringing the infection back with them from the East. Reginald's accounts of Godric's leprosy patients give us a vivid idea of the effect of the disease on the sufferer's entire life. It is very hard to catch leprosy, and the vast majority of people have a natural immunity to it, but medieval lepers were encouraged to stay away from uninfected people, which could mean that they became outcasts from their friends, families and work-colleagues. Reginald gives moving accounts of lepers cured by Godric who find themselves not only better, but able to return to their homes and lives.

As well as Godric's healing miracles, there were what we might call 'negative miracles' as well. In one case, a man called Gilbert tried to plough up some land at Finchale that Godric had never cultivated. A huge demonic raven descended on his workers and their oxen, causing the animals to stampede into the river. They were carried downstream and eventually rescued, but the leader of the human workers died twelve days later. Reginald is keen to assure us that the raven, sent from hell, that caused so much chaos could not have done so without God's permission; which presents the disturbing idea of the Almighty acting through demons. The story of the land that Godric was determined would stay uncultivated is reminiscent of modern attempts to rectify ecological damage by 'rewilding' certain areas.

Buechner's Book

It is disconcerting to read a classic of modern American literature that is set in your own little corner of England. One of the many remarkable things about County Durham is that since late in the twentieth century there have been at least two opportunities to do so. In 1997, Thomas Pynchon published his novel *Mason & Dixon*. The Dixon of the title is Jeremiah Dixon, a native of Cockfield in County Durham; consequently some scenes in Pynchon's novel take place in the so-called Land of the Prince Bishops. Nearly twenty years earlier, in 1980, Frederick Buechner brought out his much shorter novel *Godric*. It is likely that Buechner's book is one of 'the two other books, both by Americans' that Francis Rice dismisses as 'more novel than factual' in the preface to his own book on Godric, published in 1994.

Despite his very German-sounding name, Buechner is an American, who writes in English and was born in New York in 1926. *Godric* was his tenth novel, and it nearly won him a Pulitzer prize in 1981, being one of the three finalists. *A Confederacy of Dunces* by John Kennedy Toole won that year, although the author had died in 1969. Frederick Buechner, who also worked as a theologian and Presbyterian minister, should not be confused with the German playwright Georg Büchner, author of *Danton's Death*, who was born over a hundred years earlier. According to his autobiographical book *Now and Then* (1983) Buechner discovered Godric, whom he had never heard of before, in a paperback book of saints and decided that 'he was for me, my saint'.

Neither Pynchon's *Mason & Dixon* nor Buechner's *Godric* are particularly easy books to read. Though very short, *Godric* is not a novel to zip through: it is perhaps best taken slowly, with rests between the chapters. Buechner tells his story in the first person, that is, from Godric's point of view, although at times his elderly narrator refers to himself in the third person. The decision to write in Godric's voice meant that Buechner had to find a form of modern English that reflected the man and his age, an age that passed long before modern English was ever written or spoken.

As we know, Godric himself would have spoken a form of Old English, also called Anglo-Saxon, in his case perhaps tinged with dialect words from his native Norfolk, and from Durham. He would also have picked up nautical words on his travels, biblical and theological words from his reading, and ecclesiastical words from his dealings with the Church. During his life, and for a long time after it, Norman influence brought many words of French origin into the language. Slowly, English turned into something recognisable to modern English speakers and readers: the Anglo-Saxon of Godric's time is like a foreign language to us now.

Buechner's Godric sometimes slips into the third person, as if he were telling someone else's story, because for part of his life he called himself 'Deric', a contraction of 'Goderic', one possible spelling of his name. His temporary self-renaming was an attempt at evasion. The ghost of St Cuthbert had told him that Godric should live as a hermit, but he was not ready to do so quite yet. He thought he could delay the start of his hermit-life by calling himself Deric while he lived and worked as a sailor, or pirate. This idea of Buechner's is like an inversion of the story of Jonah in the Old Testament. God told Jonah to travel by sea to the city of

Nineveh to deliver a prophesy. Jonah tried to avoid his fate by staying on land. By contrast, Buechner's Godric takes to the sea to delay the commencement of his new life as a riverside hermit and prophet. In both cases, the choice God has made for the hero of the story can only be delayed, not avoided.

From page one of Buechner's novel, the language of the reformed sea-dog is suitably coarse and earthy. Godric's testicles are 'ballocks' and his penis is 'old One-eye'. As well as being fo'c'sle-foul, Godric's speech is that of a rough, semi-literate natural poet. There are many metaphors and similes, which here often manage to do their best job of allowing the reader to see familiar things afresh. In one chapter, Godric and his friend Aelred (whose name is spelled 'Ailred' here) are stranded on the roof of the former's hut when the River Wear overruns its banks. The hermit tells us that the two of them look 'like two old ravens', and he is not displeased that his biographer Reginald is not with them 'so we were spared the gaggling of a goose'. Aelred is afflicted with a terrible cough, which sounds 'like the crack of woodsmen axeing oak'.

In a paragraph in the chapter where Buechner has Aelred and Godric perched like ravens on the roof of the latter's house, Godric asks if the past is 'a sea old men can founder in before their time and drown'. Godric also compares his own nose to an anchor, his chapel to an ark and his friend Aelred to a 'sprig of hope'. The hermit also notes that the rain had turned his and Aelred's beards to seaweed. All this in the first three pages of a chapter that begins with an account of the River Wear as an angry man, or some other furious creature, driven mad by rain and melting snow.

Buechner's technicolour language brings the prose of his *Godric* close to poetry, but this poetry has none of the sweetness of, say, Edmund Spenser or Alfred Tennyson, both of whom used verse to try to evoke a lost age. The American novelist deliberately uses harsh and ugly words and phrases: getting onto their perch, the two human ravens hurt themselves; Aelred 'barked his shins' and Godric 'scraped' his own arm 'raw'. The damp pair 'croak' at each other and Aelred's bones 'clattered'. When Aelred coughs the sound is embodied in the word '*Brecch*', which is reminiscent of some of the harsh sounds uttered by the creature Gollum in Tolkein's *Lord of the Rings*.

Aelred's terrible cough is only one of the harsh symptoms of old age and infirmity that are presented in grim detail in Buechner's novel. At over a hundred years old, Godric himself is having to deal with all the health problems associated with extreme old age, in an uncomfortable environment, with none of the treatments that are now used to help our modern old folks through their later years.

While the beginning of the chapter where Godric and Aelred perch like ravens above the flood demonstrates the power of Buechner's poetic language, it also seems to be holding a sort of literary conversation with a passage from the poetry of T.S. Eliot. Perched on top of his hand-made house, Godric reflects on the nature of time:

Am I daft, or is it true there's no such thing as hours past and other hours still to pass, but all of them instead are all at once and never gone?

Compare to these lines from Eliot's *Four Quartets*:

> Time present and time past
> Are both perhaps present in time future,
> And time future contained in time past.
> If all time is eternally present
> All time is unredeemable.

Elsewhere in the novel, Buechner uses the phrase 'the skull beneath the skin' to describe the emaciated head of Godric's sister Burcwen. The phrase is from Eliot's poem *Whispers of Immortality*.

Godric's discussion of time in this passage, and his sense of all times being ever-present, connects with the unusual treatment of time in Buechner's book. To say that the story is told 'in a series of flash-backs' like some Hollywood films would be an oversimplification. There is no simple jumping between a sequence of events in the past and another in the present. Godric's mind leaps around to various periods, and his sense of the passage of time is complicated by his gift for prophecy. This means that when Godric first sees the Wear, for instance, he feels that he already knows the river: prophecy destined him for that place.

The harshness of the novel's language reflects the toughness of Buechner's Godric, and the Spartan quality of his life. He is no subtle courtier, nor one of the shy, lily-pale saints sometimes seen in paintings. It may be that the author got this idea of Godric from the account of the Finchale saint in Alban Butler's *Lives of the Saints*, which was first published in the eighteenth century. Butler tells us that Godric spoke of himself in the harshest terms, as 'the most sinful of creatures, a counterfeit hermit, an empty phantom of a religious man: lazy, slothful, proud, and imperious, abusing the charity of good people who assisted him with their alms'. In Buechner's novel, Godric has harsh things to say about other people as well, especially Reginald.

Buechner expands the traditional story of Godric's modest reluctance to cooperate with Reginald into a sort of unequal war of attrition between the two men. In the novel, Godric dislikes Reginald partly because he knows he is writing a smooth, flattering study, with all the sharp corners sanded off; not a warts-and-all exposé. By contrast, Buechner's novel exposes all of Godric's faults and sins, and as presented here these are indeed grievous.

Buechner's hermit has certainly been guilty of incest, and perhaps even rape.

The harshness of Godric's life, his language and indeed his whole world as evoked by Buechner contrasts with the hermit's conception of God and heaven. While people are often despicable, God is always praiseworthy. While the mortal world is often cruel, heaven is a source of endless mercy and comfort. While the love of other people may be a trap or a distraction, love of and for God is always worthwhile. This very medieval sense of the beauty of the spiritual world and the ugliness of mortal life will be familiar to readers who have seen a lot of the religious art of the era. Here we see horrific visions such as figures of Death and Plague depicted with the utmost grimness and realism; but we also see figures like the Virgin Mary radiant in bright, clear colours, and even with gold incorporated into the design of the picture or statue.

As a novelist writing about a real-life historical character, Buechner was surely obliged to fill in many details of his subject's life that are not supplied by the sources. Like other novelists, the American evidently used a combination of imagination and a sense of what would be right in the historical context. His Godric cannot, for instance, smoke tobacco, read a printed book, or grow tomatoes.

What the fictionalised Godric does 'off the page' of the official histories is also consistent with Buechner's own conception of his hero's character. Some of the novelist's interpolations line up with subtly-used themes in the book, such as the role of language, and the way people inhabit different roles during different parts of their lives, some of which may not suit them at all. As well as showing Godric's faults, Buechner also gives us his conception of the tragic faults and deep fault-lines in English society in the eleventh and twelfth centuries.

Godric greatly expands the sources' account of the future saint's time as a kind of steward in the house of a rich man. Buechner's version of the rich man himself is startling: this Norman aristocrat, Falkes de Granville, suffers from a complete lack of hair anywhere on his body. Vanity forces him to paint on eye-brows with ochre. He has married a beautiful Saxon girl called Hedwic who is only a child of eleven or twelve. Her much older husband regularly has sex with her, which makes him, by our standards, a serial child-molester. Godric's crushing compassion for Hedwic is well-drawn in these chapters. Later in the novel, Godric's compassion for another woman leads him into his greatest sin. In the episode where, shockingly, Godric and his sister Burcwen make love, Buechner seems to be playing with the idea that sex itself, long considered to be inherently evil by the more puritanical types of Christian, might be a blessed act.

Hedwic's odious Norman husband regards the Saxon tenants on his land as little more than the earth they live on. The whole set-up, as described by Buechner, reflects a situation that must have been seen throughout England at this time: cruel Norman masters wrecking the lives of the inhabitants of their newly-conquered land.

The cruel, callous Falkes de Granville does not deserve his wealth and power. This can also be said of Bishop Ranulf Flambard as presented in the novel, but here he is also such an amiable rogue that it is hard to resent him. A huge man who has to hunt on the back of a gigantic horse, Buechner's red-headed Bishop Flambard eats and drinks copiously, wrestles bare-chested with his servants and is enthusiastic about *grands projets* such as slum clearance, building Durham Cathedral and throwing a bridge over the Wear at Durham. Flambard's bridge lasted for nearly three hundred years, until it was wrecked by a flood in the autumn of 1400. It was then replaced by Framwellgate Bridge, which still stands. Unlike the penny-pinching de Granville, Bishop Flambard is generous to a fault, and Buechner's Godric senses a real but unconventional religious devotion at the core of his character.

The bleak household of the de Granvilles, as set out by Buechner, is an interpolation, as is an unfortunate characteristic of Godric's brother William, as written by the American. While de Granville has a kind of alopecia, William seems to be afflicted with logorrhoea, which means that he speaks copiously and endlessly, seemingly without pausing for breath. Godric explains to us why this is truly an affliction: not only is everyone constantly worn out by listening to William; his problem isolates him because he cannot pause to listen to anyone else, and thus enjoy some meaningful contact. This makes him pitifully lonely, like his siblings Burcwen and Godric: loneliness and isolation are also important themes in the novel.

While William's tiresome loquaciousness and the distressing details of the de Granville household have little basis in the original sources for Godric, Buechner includes elements that are prominent features of the hermit's legend. These include the saint's iron jacket; here not made of chain-mail, nor any kind of battle-armour, but something cobbled together by a blacksmith, which looks more like pots and pans than knightly gear.

With its vivid language, powerful characterisations and striking insights into the saint's thought-processes, Buechner's Godric novel succeeds in presenting a convincing picture of the hermit of Finchale, of his age, and of the landscapes against which his life unfolded. The book's strong sense of the Wearside setting is a reminder that, though the twelfth century and its attitudes may be a long way in the past, some of the English landscape continues in a state not too dissimilar to the condition it was in when the Normans ruled the country. Global warming may, however, cause riverside places like Finchale to sink permanently under the rising waters, and lose their ancient flora and fauna.

For a short novel like Buechner's *Godric*, the depiction of a striking character like the saintly hero's is achievement enough. It is, however, possible to imagine a longer, more comprehensive work of fiction, something on the lines of Ken Follett's 1989 epic novel *The Pillars of the Earth*, based around Godric and giving us much more detail about the man and his age. Follett's novel, which was rediscovered, and received a lot of belated acclaim, early in the twenty-first century, stretches to over a thousand pages in paperback and is set in the period Godric shared with King Henry I, Henry II, Thomas Becket and the Christian Kingdom of Jerusalem. *The Pillars of the Earth* was made into a TV drama series and even a computer game.

The novel's rediscovery spurred Follett, previously known for modern-set thrillers, to write sequels and a prequel, and, in the opinion of many readers, these works sit above many other modern English-language historical novels set in the twelfth century. Such works can serve as an entertaining way to acquire knowledge about a historical period. In English, this particular trail was blazed by the Scottish novelist Walter Scott, whose best-known book, *Ivanhoe* (1819) was also set in the twelfth century. In fact Frederick Buechner's account of the twelfth century scene in his Godric novel is so impressionistic and lacking in explanatory detail that the author added a two-page historical note at the end, giving the bones of Godric's story, whereas the novel itself might be said to be the muscle and sinew.

It is likely that, to achieve the appropriate kind of 'grand sweep', a more conventional type of historical novel centred on the figure of Godric would spend many chapters on the future saint's life as a Mediterranean pirate, getting involved at the edges of great historical moments such as King Baldwin I's escape to Jaffa.

Buechner's depiction of this episode begins with the briefest mention of the lost battle which left Baldwin in great danger and almost alone, and which it is clear that Godric did not witness.

Most of Buechner's account of Baldwin's rescue consists of impressions of what Godric saw and heard at the time, at Arsuf: looting; frenzied, panicked praying; the sound of 'fearful keening'; a burning church; men loading camels with all their worldly goods. Into this chaos steps Baldwin, a tall knight wearing a golden coronet, speaking with 'a voice of brass'.

Buechner's version of Baldwin characterises himself as the earthly saviour of Christian Jerusalem: 'If I'm not there, it falls for sure' he says, meaning Jaffa, the city's port. Then 'the ungodly Turk will foul the places sacred to Our Lord'. Having appealed to the Saxon pirates' religious loyalty, Baldwin then involves them in a ritual where they kiss the cross-shaped top of his sword, and embrace him, tearfully, 'like brothers'.

Judging from what history has remembered about Baldwin, this is just the sort of thing he might have done. Whether this odd procedure had any real meaning for his royal majesty is not something on which Buechner cares to speculate. In any case, the novel's version of Baldwin seems to have procured a free rescue from Godric and Mouse, his fellow-pirate, when presumably the two men could have charged a fortune for this service to any of the rich commoners who were trying to escape from Arsuf. In the end, their only reward is the realisation that 'a pair of ragged Saxon rogues' had cheated the enemy.

What Godric Was

Frederick Buechner's novel *Godric* is only one interpretation of the hermit, his life and his times. The American's work is partly based on a reading of Reginald's biography, but the Durham monk's text should also be regarded as just another interpretation. We have seen how Godric's friend and biographer seems to re-use elements from the hagiographies of other saints in his *Life* of the hermit. This does not necessarily mean that he made up stories relating to Godric, to make him seem more like Saint Anthony of Egypt, or Saint Cuthbert. He may only have selected, from a mass of tales which he was prepared to believe were true, those which, if set down with care, would make Godric look like a saint after the approved pattern. This might look like an attempt to 'sanitise' his subject: if so it is possible to see Buechner's fictional interpretation as the insanitary version; the hidden history and the shocking truth.

The power of selection, of 'editing' a story, may have been used by Reginald, perhaps without even thinking about it, when he came to relate Godric's healing miracles. Over two hundred of these got into his book, but we know that many, many people looking for a miraculous cure visited Godric at Finchale during his long life. Even if only one ailing, hopeful pilgrim per week visited Godric during his nearly sixty years living as a hermit, he would still have seen over three thousand sick people, or people living with disabilities or impairments. If he only cured the two hundred or so whom Reginald mentions, then his success-rate was not much more than a measly six percent. Even if only one invalid a month turned up begging for a cure, then Godric was only really helping around a quarter of them. If we remember that many health conditions are 'self-limiting' and clear up without treatment, this success-rate seems even less impressive.

It would probably not have occurred to Reginald to do the sums on which the paragraph above is based: if he ever did, he never wrote down the results in a form that is still extant. If nothing else, accounts of thousands of fruitless visits to Godric would make for many monotonous and even depressing pages of manuscript. If Reginald ever had such doubts, he most likely kept them to himself. He was, after all, supposed to be a soldier for Christ, fighting heresy, doubt and disbelief with the Good News that is the heart of the Christian message. We can picture him, quill poised, eyes ready to see, and ears to hear, only what he believed believers needed to read about.

While Buechner and Reginald both give us highly selective interpretations of Godric, a similarly partial impression can be obtained by modern visitors to Finchale. Here, at times, there is a healing stillness that recalls certain gardens in Japan, the serene design of which is influenced by Zen Buddhist ideas.

There is an ancient Buddhist sutra, or scripture, the original of which probably pre-dates any Christian text, that comprises a series of verses directing those who seek enlightenment to live like the rhinoceros. The author of the *Rhinoceros Sutra* was probably thinking of the solitary, forest-dwelling Indian rhino. Although the poem is very ancient, and comes from a very different culture, it seems to map out at least some of the parameters of Godric's life, and the lives of many hermits, in the Christian tradition and beyond. If nothing else, it is a reminder that Christianity does not hold the copyright on holy people who seek solitude in the wilderness.

The Sutra insists on the merits of changing one's appearance as a kind of gateway to a new way of life, but whereas Godric wore a black monk's habit and a mail shirt, and grew his beard and hair long, the Buddhist hermit is advised to shave off his hair and beard and don an ochre robe.

The *Rhinoceros Sutra* is careful to set out the allurements of the world, which the ascetic must choose to renounce. These include good food and female companionship, the latter described here in terms of seductive tresses and the look of gold bangles on a shapely arm. They also include family – parents and children, and all friends, apart from perhaps one true spiritual friend, who is wise in the ways of the Dhamma, or teachings of the Buddha. Perhaps for Godric his most valuable friend, the man who acted as guide for the most important part of his spiritual journey, was Prior Roger of Durham.

The Sutra offers a number of eye-catching similes for people who have attained enlightenment in the solitary life. They are said to be like bamboo sprouts, too small to be entangled with other plants. They are like free-grazing wild deer, or a tree that has shed its leaves. They are like a king who has renounced his kingdom, an elephant who has split off from the herd, or the wind, that cannot be caught in a net.

For some Buddhists, part of the motivation for seeking enlightenment is the possibility that the truly enlightened person will shed pain along with the 'entanglements' of life. Yes, friendship and family are blessings, but they can also bring pain, for instance when a beloved friend or family member dies or is sick, or when discord breaks out and love starts to turn bitter.

The Sutra's grooming advice to the would-be ascetic, to shave off his hair and beard, is phrased in such a way that the reader understands that these hairy accessories are outward and visible signs of the life of the family man, or householder. Perhaps the rhino-ascetic has lived a full life, replete with family, friends, a house and a modicum of wealth, and is now casting these aside, together with his locks and his whiskers. In this way the Buddhist ascetic is similar to Godric, who certainly lived a full life before he came to Finchale, but there is no hint that Godric ever had a wife or children.

Paraphrasing the Persian poet Saadi Shirazi in his book *Walden*, Henry Thoreau explores the concept of freedom. A wise man is asked, why is the cypress the only tree called *azad*, or free? The wise man answers, because it bears no fruit, and is not altered by the seasons, 'and of this nature are the *azads*, or religious independents'. As a man who fathered no children, Godric was free like the fruitless cypress, but one cannot help lamenting the loss to the human species of his tough, long-lived DNA.

As a Christian ascetic, Godric seems to have spent a lot of time trying to make his experience in the wilderness as bitter as possible: how could he attain to the Zen-like calm of a serene statue of the Buddha, when he was up to his chin in a freezing river? Like many Christian saints and solitaries, the hermit of Finchale actively sought pain, rather than its opposite. In the Sutra, there is a recognition that there are pains in the solitary life that have to be endured – 'wind and sun, horseflies and snakes' – but, I think, no feeling that these need to be actively sought out. There was an urgency about Godric's quest, a very Christian sense that time was running out, despite the fact that, as a centenarian, Godric's time took a very long time to pass by.

The *Rhinoceros Sutra* could be read as a call to an extreme form of the 'down-sizing' that many people in the West have embraced in recent years. Hard work at a stressful job may bring in plenty of money, but 'quiet enjoyment', a concept enshrined in English law, can be hard to find. A hectic social life may make one feel popular, but how many of the people who drank your champagne at that last big party are valued friends? Better to take a year off, to 'cultivate one's garden', in Voltaire's phrase, or switch to part-time work, or a less stressful job, and find some peace. On a still day at Finchale, it is easy to feel how Godric could have found serenity here, but there is evidence that this was not what he was looking for at all. In his knightly chain-mail shirt, he was a warrior for Christ – a gruff, thick-skinned rhino, forever charging at demons and temptations.

For literary Americans, the *locus classicus* of the determined down-sizer is Walden Pond, and Thoreau's book *Walden* is the classic text. It would be easy for modern readers to link Thoreau's *Walden* and Yeats's poem *The Lake Isle of Innisfree* to Godric, and to set their mental picture of the hermit of Finchale into this frame. But Thoreau in particular took to his self-built waterside retreat for reasons that Godric would probably have found incomprehensible.

We might think that Thoreau was thinking about someone like Godric when he wrote that 'with respect to luxuries and comforts, the wisest have ever lived a more simple and meagre life than the poor'. But Godric was trying to attain something other than wisdom, though wisdom may have been a by-product of his search for personal salvation and deeper communion with the spirit of heaven. As he grew older, the hermit of Finchale looked for ways to share his own spiritual gifts and insights – hence the waning of the gruff, unsociable Godric and the waxing of that paradoxical thing, the hermit who was always ready to welcome visitors.

Thoreau was evidently looking to live and think like 'the wisest' with their 'simple and meagre' lives, and the cypress-like 'religious independents' of Saadi Shirazi. But he seems to have believed that simplicity itself, something like Yeats's 'small cabin' 'of clay and wattles made', would bring wisdom along with it. He even attached spiritual significance to the business of building his own little hut, and growing his own beans, and declared that:

I went to the woods because I wished to live deliberately, to front only the essential facts of life, and see if I could not learn what it had to teach, and not, when I came to die, discover that I had not lived.

By contrast, Godric was more interested in the afterlife than this life, and may have found Thoreau's reliance on Nature (with a capital 'N') as a key to the spiritual life nothing more than paganism. 'Every morning was a cheerful invitation to make my life of equal simplicity, and I may say innocence, with Nature herself,' wrote the American, and followed that sentence with something more specifically pagan: 'I have been as sincere a worshipper of Aurora as the Greeks'. He goes on to tell us that 'I got up early and bathed in the pond; that was a religious exercise, and one of the best things which I did'. Godric too immersed himself in cold water, but surely he would never have thought of this activity as a 'religious exercise' in itself.

Thoreau's time by Walden Pond had a political and economic aspect as well. He spent many pages of *Walden* lambasting the capitalists of nearby Concord, Massachusetts, who wore themselves out accumulating wealth, but, he implied, were never really contented, and had no time for themselves. By trying to 'reduce' life 'to its lowest terms' Thoreau hoped to have more time to, for instance, sit all morning at the door of his hut, doing nothing at all. To Godric such idleness would have looked like a snare of the devil, and it is likely that he viewed personal contentment in the same way.

It may be that to put our picture of Godric into a Buddhist frame, or to associate him with nineteenth-century notions of the transcendence of nature, is just as inappropriate as turning a modern scientific microscope on this twelfth-century hermit, saint, mystic and miracle-worker. Strict followers of the scientific approach might not hesitate to doubt Godric's success-rate as a healer, or to attribute his waking visions to schizophrenia. They might also suggest that he mortified his flesh not out of devotion to God, but masochism, or because of his ever-present awareness of some terrible crime in his past, for which he felt he had to do penance.

The author of *Walden* was disturbed by the steam-trains, with raging fires in their bellies, that he could hear from his philosophical hermitage on Walden Pond. Perhaps he was trying to reduce his own inner flame to a gentle smoulder, for the sake of his spiritual, psychological and physical health. His aim is reminiscent of the target set in the Buddha's famous Fire Sermon, in which he proposed that Buddhist monks should try to turn down the heat of their passions by liberating themselves from the influence of their senses. Godric, by contrast, strove to keep his spiritual fire white-hot.

Appendix: Godric's Songs

A SONG OF THANKSGIVING

Crist and sainte marie swa on scamel me iledde
þat ic on þis erðe ne silde wid mine bare fote itredie

(Thanks to the support of Christ and Mary
Propping me up, my feet never touch the ground.)

TO THE VIRGIN MARY

Sainte marie uirgine
moder ihesu cristes nazarene
onfo schild help þin godric
onfang bring heȝilich wið þe in godes riche

Sainte marie xristes bur
maidenes clenhad moderes flur
dilie min sinne rix in min mod
bring me to winne wið þe selfd God

(Oh virgin Saint Mary
Mother of Jesus of Nazareth
Protect and aid your Godric
And take him with you
Into God's kingdom.

Mary, pure flower of virgins,
Maiden, bower of Christ,
Possess me, erase my sins,
Bring me the joy of God.)

SAINT NICHOLAS

Sainte Nicholaes godes druð
tymbre us faire scone hus
At þi burth at þi bare
Sainte nicholaes bring vs wel þare

(Saint Nicholas, beloved of God;
Build us a fine, strong house,
And at the time of birth and death
Saint Nicholas, shelter us there.)

Bibliography

Aelred of Rievaulx: *The Historical Works*, trans. J.P. Freeman, Cictercian, 2008

Aelred of Rievaulx: *The Lives of the Northern Saints*, trans. J.P. Freeland, Cistercian, 2006

Athanasius of Alexandria: *Life of Saint Anthony*, trans. H. Ellershaw, from *Nicene and Post-Nicene Fathers*, Second Series, Vol. 4. Edited by Philip Schaff and Henry Wace, Christian Literature Publishing Co., 1892

Athanasius of Alexandria: *The Life of Antony*, trans. Tim Vivian and Apostolos N. Athanassakis, Cistercian, 2003

Bede: *The Ecclesiastical History of the English People*, Oxford, 1999

Benedict of Nursia: *The Rule of Saint Benedict* (trans. Abbot Parry), Gracewing, 1990

Bernard of Clairvaux: *Selected Works*, Paulist, 1987

Besant, Walter: *Jerusalem, the City of Herod and Saladin*, Richard Bentley and Son, 1871

Bobko, Jane (ed.): *Vision: The Life and Music of Hildegard von Bingen*, Penguin, 1995

Boyd, Anne: *The Monks of Durham*, Cambridge, 1975

Buechner, Frederick: *Godric*, Harper, 1980

Cannuyer, Christian: *Coptic Egypt: The Christians of the Nile*, Thames & Hudson, 2001

Colgrave, Bertram: *Two Lives of Saint Cuthbert*, Cambridge, 1985

Comnena, Anna: *The Alexiad* (trans. E.R.A. Sewter), Penguin, 1969

A Complete Guide to Finchale Priory, Thomas Caldcleugh

Coulton, G.G.: *Social Life in Britain from the Conquest to the Reformation*, Cambridge, 1918

Dante (trans. D.L. Sayers): *The Divine Comedy: Hell*, Penguin, 1977

Edgington, Susan B.: *Baldwin I of Jerusalem, 1100-1118*, Routledge, 2019

Ellis, Simon P.: *Graeco-Roman Egypt*, Shire, 1992

Evans, G.R.: *Bernard of Clairvaux*, Oxford, 2000

Görg, Peter H.: *The Desert Fathers*, trans. Michael J. Miller, Ignatius, 2011

Happe, Peter (ed.): *English Mystery Plays*, Penguin, 1975

Hegge, Robert: *The Legend of St. Cuthbert*, George Garbutt, 1816

Henry of Huntingdon: *A History of the English People 1000-1154*, trans. Diana Greenway, Oxford, 2002

Hunter Blair, C.H. (ed.) *Archaeologia Aeliana*, Society of Antiquaries of Newcastle upon Tyne, 1930 (article by H.H.E. Craster on Ranulf Flambard, pp. 33-57)

John of Wurzburg (trans. Aubrey Stewart): *Description of the Holy Land,* Palestine Pilgrims' Text Society, 1890

Kendall, A; *Medieval Pilgrims*, Wayland, 1970

Knowles, David: *Saints and Scholars*, Cambridge, 1962

McKeating, Henry: *Ezekiel*, Sheffield Academic Press, 1993

Meade, Dorothy: *The Parish Church of St Giles Durham City* (leaflet), 2016

Miller, Timothy S. and Nesbitt, John W.: *Walking Corpses: Leprosy in Byzantium and the Medieval West*, Cornell, 2014

Oman, C.W.C.: *The Byzantine Empire*, T. Fisher Unwin, 1902

Orderic Vitalis: *The Ecclesiastical History of England and Normandy* (Vol. IV, trans. Thomas Forester), Bohn, 1853

Pandita, K.N.: *Ibn Sina (Avicenna)*, University of Kashmir, Srinagar, 1981

Reginald of Durham: *Life and Miracles of St. Godric*, Surtees Society, 1845

Rice, Francis: *The Hermit of Finchale: The Life of Saint Godric*, Pentland, 1994

Runciman, Steven: *A History of the Crusades 2: The Kingdom of Jerusalem*, Penguin, 1965

Ryder, Peter: *Finchale Priory*, English Heritage, 2000

Sebag Montefiore,, Simon: *Jerusalem: The Biography*, Weidenfeld & Nicolson, 2011

Simeon of Durham: *The Historical Works of Simeon of Durham* (trans. J. Stevenson), Seeleys, 1855

Smith, J.F.J.: *The Abridged Life of St. Godric and the Tragedy of Finchale Priory*, J.F.J. Smith

Squire, Aelred: *Aelred of Rievaulx*, SPCK, 1969

Stevenson, Joseph (trans.): *The Church Historians of England, Vol. IV part I*, Seeleys, 1856

Stewart, Aubrey (ed.): *Anonymous Pilgrims (11th and 12th Centuries)*, Palestine Pilgrims' Text Society, 1894

Talbot, C.H. (trans.): *The Life of Christina of Markyate*, Oxford, 1959

Thoreau, Henry David: *Walden*, Penguin, 2016

Tyerman, Christopher (ed.): *Chronicles of the First Crusade*, Penguin, 2011

Vertot, L De: *The History of the Knights Hospitallers*, J. Christie, 1818

Waddell, Helen: *The Desert Fathers*, Fontana, 1962

Webb, Diana: *Pilgrimage in Medieval England*, Hambledon and London, 2000

Weinandy, Thomas G.: *Athanasius: A Theological Introduction*, Ashgate, 2007

Williams, Joan: *Mappa Mundi and the Chained Library: Treasures of Hereford Cathedral*, Jarrold, 1999

Wingate, Peter and Wingate, Richard: *The Penguin Medical Encyclopaedia*, Penguin, 1988

Wood, Michael: *The Story of England*, Penguin, 2011

Yeats, W.B.: *Selected Poems*, Penguin, 2000

For more books from the Langley Press, please visit our website at:

www.langleypress.co.uk

Made in United States
Troutdale, OR
09/15/2025

34548610R00080